COLLECTION

Big Data

SIMPLIFYING BIG DATA

IN 7 CHAPTERS

Prof. Marcão - Marcus Vinícius Pinto

Disclaimer:

Please note that the information contained in this document is for educational and entertainment purposes only. Every effort has been made to provide complete, accurate, up-to-date, and reliable information. No warranty of any kind is express or implied.

By reading this text, the reader agrees that under no circumstances is the author liable for any losses, direct or indirect, incurred as a result of the use of the information contained in this book, including, but not limited to, errors, omissions, or inaccuracies.

ISBN: 9798310847767

Publishing imprint: Independently published

Summary.

1   Foreword.

Big Data. What once seemed like a distant concept restricted to technology giants, has now become an essential part of the daily lives of companies, governments, and even individuals. But, with so much information and technical jargon, where to start? How to transform this sea of data into something understandable and applicable?

It was with this question in mind that Simplifying Big Data into 7 Chapters. This book is an accessible, practical, and comprehensive guide designed for those who want to understand Big Data in a clear and hassle-free way. Whether you are an experienced professional or someone who is taking your first steps in the area, you will find the answers you are looking for here.

1.1   Who will benefit from this book?

- Managers and organizational leaders: In the business world, data-driven decision-making is no longer a differential and has become a necessity. This book helps leaders understand the fundamentals of Big Data and apply them strategically in their operations, from crisis management to process optimization.

- Data analysts and data scientists: For professionals in the field, the book provides insights into architecture, tools, and trends, as well as exploring practical examples that can be applied in everyday life, such as predictive analytics and data governance.

- Entrepreneurs and small business professionals: We demystify the use of Big Data for small operations, showing how it can be used to increase efficiency, improve the customer experience, and identify new market opportunities.

- Students and technology enthusiasts: If you are curious to understand the role of Big Data in digital transformation and the advancement of artificial intelligence, this book is the ideal starting point.

1.2   What will you find in this book?

With a structured approach, we have divided the content into seven chapters that connect theory and practice:

- We start with the basic concepts: what Big Data is, the famous 5 Vs and how distributed computing has revolutionized the way we deal with data.

- We explore the fundamental steps for the success of Big Data projects, accompanied by real examples in areas such as health, environment and retail.

- We debunk common myths and present trends for the future, helping you stay ahead of the curve.

- We dive into Hadoop, one of the pillars of Big Data, explaining its architecture and ecosystem in a simple and straightforward way.

- And, of course, we address data analysis, its techniques and practical applications, as well as the importance of data governance.

Each chapter is built to offer a complete and integrated view, allowing you to understand not only the "what" and "how" but also the "why" behind Big Data.

1.3   Why should you buy this book?

This book is more than an introduction to Big Data. It is an indispensable tool for those who want to turn data into value. By purchasing Simplifying Big Data in 7 Chapters, you will have access to clear language, solid concepts and practical examples that bridge the gap between the technical and the strategic.

But this work is only part of a larger journey. As part of the Big Data Collection, it connects to other volumes that explore advanced aspects such as predictive analytics, machine learning algorithms, and systems integration strategies. Each book in the collection delves into an essential component, providing a holistic and practical view of the universe of Big Data and artificial intelligence.

Whether you're a manager, analyst, or tech enthusiast, this collection is at your disposal on Amazon, ready to elevate your knowledge and boost your bottom line.

Get ready to tap into the power of data. Your journey starts now!

Happy reading!
Prof. Marcão

Prof. Marcão - Marcus Vinícius Pinto

M.Sc. in Information Technology
Writer on topics of information technology,
artificial intelligence, data governance,
information architecture, and humanities.
Discover my books on Amazon!

2 Big Data. Big what?

Big Data has become "the" most important technological trend of the last decade and has the potential to alter the world of science and information technology and impact companies in an absolutely unprecedented way, completely transforming their business models (Gens, 2012).

Big Data, contrary to what it may seem, is not a single platform (Chen et al., 2012) (Manyika, 2011), but rather a mix of data processing and management technologies that have developed over time.

We know that managing and analyzing data has always brought numerous benefits to companies, but we also know that it has always brought great challenges and investments.

In the days when commerce was done in a small shop or door to door, it was easy to manage the needs of customers and keep them loyal. It was possible to sell the same product for years and years. Customers felt prestigious for the simple fact of having an attentive and cordial supplier.

With the advancement of technology, with the Internet present in every corner, no matter how remote it may be, customers have evolved and it is increasingly difficult to retain them and keep them satisfied.

To survive and gain a competitive advantage, companies have been adding new products and services to their portfolios more and more quickly. The consequence of this is the generation of a huge variety of research, controls, processes and constraints.

The great advantage, and it is really great, of Big Data is that it provides companies with specific tools for storing, managing and manipulating large amounts of data at the right time, with the right precision and with the necessary speed so that managers and users of all markets and hierarchical levels have their decision-making processes maximized (Helbing, 2014).

To assimilate the potential of Big Data, it is necessary to keep in mind that:

Data must be processed in order to support the business needs for which a software solution has been designed, developed and implemented.

Users are looking for more and more novelty and speed in satisfying their wants and needs, forcing companies to run so as not to be left behind. It is important to be aware of the various issues that need to be analyzed before implementation and face them, because whoever comes out ahead will dominate the market.

But not everything is rosy.

Big Data is not a *plug and play* solution. Its implementation requires a sophisticated infrastructure that needs to be adjusted to the needs of its users. Its implementation requires a lot of planning and study.

It is important to keep in mind several issues that need to be analyzed before implementation, such as:

- What Big Data architecture is needed for your company's challenges?

- Does your *data center*[1] support this type of technology?

- Does the company use DW[2] and is replacing one technology with another?

- What are the security implications of your data in Big Data?

- Does your company use cloud computing?

- Can your strategic and analytical needs be met by DW?

Data, according to Helbing (2014), is becoming, in this context, not a new oil capable of supplying wealth by itself, but a source of challenges that need to be structured and sustained by reliable processes to become a source of profitability.

The complexity of databases today means that companies have to deal with relational databases, NoSQL, documents, images, application messages, emails, photos, videos and a multitude of other media and platforms to keep their customers satisfied.

Other challenges in data management are emerging every day, such as social media data, clickstream, mobile connections, connected databases.

Big Data allows you to process data in a way that was unthinkable until recently. It makes it possible to analyze data patterns to:

---

[1] The *Data Center* is an environment designed to house servers and other *hardware* components, such as data storage systems (storages) and network assets (switches, routers). Its objective is to ensure the availability of equipment for the information systems that guarantee the continuity of the company's business.

[2] Data warehouse – DW. Data Warehouse is a type of data management system designed to enable and support business intelligence (BI) activities, especially advanced analytics. DWs are intended solely for performing advanced queries and analysis, and often contain large amounts of historical data.

- Maximize city management efforts.

- Fraud prevention.

- Conducting experiments.

- Fault detection.

- Traffic management in large urban centers.

- Improved customer satisfaction.

- Improved product quality.

And here we are citing just a few examples.

This is the right time to acquire mastery over this technology because there are few professionals with specialized knowledge and most companies, impacted by the realization of the advantages, challenges, investment needs and culture change are looking for professionals to train their teams (Armstrong, 2016).

At the same time that information technology professionals are discovering this new job niche, companies are facing a growing number of data available for their market analysis and are realizing that the technologies they use are insufficient for the new challenges of the Internet.

The emerging technologies and tools that form the core of this book can help you understand and unleash the tremendous power of Big Data, which is changing the world as we know it.

In this book you will learn how the proposal to use Big Data to transform huge amounts of data into valuable information is and how your company can use this data in the best way. In addition, I will provide you with tips and updates on changes in software, hardware, and data processing methodologies for data analysis.

So welcome to this technological trend called Big Data.

2.1   But what is Big Data?

IT professionals are used to dealing with databases with different structures, different manipulation languages and different communication networks. However, each architecture has its application and constitutes a solution to a certain class of problems, dealing with certain data sources.

In the world of the internet, with different sources of data that need to be managed, researched and analyzed independently for a certain purpose, the problem is escalated to impossible levels, ceasing to be a solution and becoming a huge problem.

Thus, we can say that being faced with so much data, with such varied forms, it is impossible to think of "traditional" management. New challenges call for new solutions. Big Data is "the" new solution.

It is possible to think of the evolution of data management as isolated stages of technological advancement. According to Stonebraker (2012), these stages are not necessarily an evolution of the previous stage. However, whether unpublished or derivative, most of the technological advances of the stages are based on their precursors.

Although the advances of DBMS[3] and data architecture management approaches are seen as the evolutionary foundations of the information world, it is necessary to understand this evolution in the context of software + hardware + data. For Hilbert (2013):

"Technological revolutions combined with cost reductions, considering scenarios of reduction in the size of storage devices with a large increase in the volume of recorded data and high gains in computational processing speed, have made it possible to develop new

---

[3] Database Management Systems - DBMS is a software for database management, which allows you to create, modify and insert elements. The term has its origin in the English Data Base Management System, or simply DBMS.

perspectives and the emergence of opportunities in the universe of the intersection of platforms and data sources, generating new management products."

While all these technology factors converge, we experience a complete transformation in the way we manage and use data. Big Data is the most recent trend to emerge from all these factors.

It is defined as any type of data analysis platform that has these five characteristics:

- Extremely large volumes.

- Technological architecture with extremely high processing speed capacity.

- Wide range of processed data types.

- Data with potential value for the company

- Data with high reliability.

2.2   5 Vs of Big Data

Big Data experts have developed a theory called the 5 Vs (Subramaniam, 2020).

- Volume.

  - The concept of volume in Big Data is evidenced by internet traffic composed of e-mail exchanges, banking transactions, interactions on social networks, call records and data traffic on telephone lines.

  - It is estimated that the total volume of data circulating on the internet in 2021 is 340 Exabytes per year.

  - Every day 2.9 quintillion bytes are created in the form of

data, currently 90% of all data that is present in the world was created in the last 3 years (Manyika (2011)).

- It is also important to understand that the concept of volume is a variable that depends on the time considered, that is, what is great today, may be nothing tomorrow. (Lohr, 2012) (Ohlhorst, 2012).

- In the 90s, a Terabyte (1012 bytes) was considered Big Data.

- Speed.

  - Would you cross a street blindfolded if the last information you had was a photograph taken of the circulating traffic from 5 minutes ago? Probably not, as the photograph from 5 minutes ago is irrelevant now. You need to know the current conditions so that you can cross the street safely. (Forbes, 2012). The same logic applies to companies, as they need current data about their business, that is, speed.

  - According to Taurion (2013), the importance of speed is such that at some point there must be a tool capable of analyzing data in real time.

  - Currently, data is analyzed only after it is stored, but the time spent for storage itself already disqualifies this type of analysis as a 100% real-time analysis.

  - Information is power (Rogers, 2010), and therefore, the speed with which this information is obtained is a competitive advantage for companies.

  - Speed can limit the operation of many businesses, when we use the credit card, for example, if we do not get an approval of the purchase in a few seconds we usually think of using another payment method. It is the operator losing a business opportunity due to the failure in the speed of transmission and analysis of the buyer's data.

- Daily and long-term analyses of Big Data can be done. Both cases can be useful for the person responsible for this area to know how to identify the speed with which the analyzes need to be done.

- Variety.

  - Volume is just the beginning of the challenges of this new technology, if we have a huge volume of data, we also have a huge variety of it.

  - Have you ever thought about the amount of information dispersed on social networks? Facebook, Twitter, among others, have a vast and distinct field of information being offered in public at all times.

  - We can observe the variety of data in emails, social networks, photographs, audios, phones and credit cards. (McAffe et al, 2012). We can get infinite points of view on the same information.

  - Companies that can capture variety, whether from sources or criteria, add more value to the business.

  - Big Data scales the variety of information in the following ways:

    o Structured data: is stored in databases, sequenced in tables. Example: tables or forms filled in by customers.

    o Semi-structured data: follows heterogeneous patterns, is more difficult to identify because it can follow several patterns. For example, if an image is taken from a smartphone, it will have some structured attributes like geotag, device ID, and timestamp. Once stored, images can also be tagged as 'pet' or 'dog' to provide a structure.

- o Unstructured data: This is a mix of data from diverse sources such as images, audios, and online documents. Example: messages, photos, videos.

- Out of these 3 categories, it is estimated that up to 90% of all data in the world is in the form of unstructured data.

- Truthfulness.

  - One in 3 leaders do not trust the data they receive (IBM, 2014).

  - To reap good results from the Big Data process, it is necessary to obtain truthful data, according to reality.

  - The concept of speed, already analyzed, is linked to the concept of veracity due to the constant need for real-time analysis. This means that the data match the reality at that time, as past data cannot be considered true data for the later moment.

  - The relevance of the data collected is as important as the volume, as there is no point in having quantity without quality.

  - Checking the collected data for adequacy and relevance to the purpose of the analysis is a key point to obtain data that adds value to the process.

  - Not all of the data collected is true. This is the case, for example, of fake news4, which can spread quickly on the Internet.

- Value.

    - It is necessary to focus on guiding the business, as the value of collecting and analyzing data is measured by the benefit it will bring to the business.

    - It is not feasible to carry out the entire Big Data process if you do not have questions that help the business in a realistic way.

    - In the same way, it is important to be aware of the costs involved in this operation, the added value of all this work developed, collection, storage and analysis of all this data has to compensate for the financial costs involved (Taurion, 2013).

    - Information can have special value for a company's marketing campaigns. The idea is for the team to evaluate which data is more or less valuable and apply it in their strategies according to their degree of importance.

As you can see, Big Data is indispensable for success and improvements in several areas of your company. It should be seen as a kind of compass that every entrepreneur should use to get to know themselves, their audience, and their competition.

---

[4] Fake News is fake news published by media outlets as if it were real information. In evidence since 2016, its popularization was due to the US elections that defined Donald Trump as the 45th president of the United States.

Big Data is important because it provides means for the company to store, manage, and process large amounts of data according to its needs (Glass et al. (2015). But realize that it is important to keep in mind that Big Data is the result of the evolution of data management and it is essential to understand how the last 50 years of maturation of the technology determined the appearance of this new technology.

Companies have been experiencing a multitude of problems in their data management for some time now, as they have evolved from the stage where DW technology was quite sufficient.

Today, companies deal with more data from more sources than previously thought possible. All this data is known as "the new oil", but without the proper tools the drilling of this "oil" does not produce wealth.

In these new times, the challenges of data management technology are:

1. How does the company work with huge amounts of data in order to consider it as a useful collection?

2. How to give meaning to this immensity of data if it is not possible to recognize the patterns to make them meaningful for the company's business processes and decisions?

2.3   The concept of Big Data.

To get a sense of the evolution of something, it is necessary to identify significant differences between the results of the various versions of that something. For example, when it comes to the evolution of automobiles, we have distinct phases, starting with animal-drawn vehicles, evolving to steam cars, moving on to simple combustion engines, reaching the current electric autonomous vehicles. It is easy to understand the different stages of the automotive product.

Data management is no different. Taking as a focus of validation of the difference between the generations of managers the way to solve the problems then posed, it is possible to affirm that each generation evolved due to cause and effect factors.

When a new technology hits the market, it establishes new ways of working. A good example was the arrival on the market of relational database technology. Due to the huge differences between this proposal and previous solutions, it was necessary for companies to look for ways to adapt to make good use of their resources.

The previous generation, dominated by[5] IBM's[6] VSAM, was quickly abandoned due to the potential for processing much larger databases with more modular and versatile programs.

The technological generation based on object orientation was faced with new forms of programming, but there was no real evolution in the management of databases.

A new scenario was posed by the storage of unstructured data in which it was necessary for information technology professionals to become familiar with analysis tools based on natural language, to generate useful results for the companies' businesses.

---

[5] VIRTUAL STORAGE ACCESS METHOD - VSAM. The Virtual Storage Access Method. It is a file management method that is mostly used on mainframes, but also on PCs. VSAM speeds up access to file data by using a reverse index of records attached to files. This index is called the B+ tree.

[6] International Business Machines Corporation (IBM) is a United States company focused on the computer industry. IBM manufactures and sells hardware and software, offers infrastructure services, hosting services, and consulting services in areas ranging from large computers to nanotechnology. It was nicknamed "Big Blue" for adopting blue as its official corporate color, in Portuguese "Big Blue".

In parallel, the evolution of search engines has given rise to tools that aimed to generate profit from the indexing and retrieval of significant data in the internet scenario.

This evolutionary process started before the turn of the century culminated at the point where we are with the arrival of Big Data. An essential characteristic of this evolutionary process is the fact that from one generation to the next there was no substitution of tools, methodologies and concepts, but rather the generation of a range of alternatives for different problems. Big Data is a derivative of this range of solutions.

Returning to the context of technology in the mid-1960s, when computing presented itself as a processing alternative in the market of commercial companies, data was stored in simple files, magnetic tapes, which had primary structures.

When companies needed more complex results to support their decision-making processes or their production and product delivery chain, it took a superhuman effort to create value from these files.

In the 1970s, Peter Chen revolutionized data managers by proposing the relational data model that imposed a new structure and aimed at improving computer parks.

However, the main differentiator of this approach was the introduction of abstraction levels through the structured query language, SQL[7], and report generators.

---

[77] SQL stands for "Structured Query Language" which means, in Portuguese, Structured Query Language, a standard data management language that interacts with the main databases based on the relational model. Some of the main systems that use SQL are: MySQL, Oracle, Firebird, Microsoft Access, PostgreSQL (open source), HSQLDB (open source and written in Java).

The relational model, developed by Charles Bachman and James Martin, consolidated a way of thinking, working, and processing data that met the growing needs of companies that, at that time, were present in several countries becoming transnational.

This technology allowed business managers to examine stratified, segmented, and cross-referenced information such as the number of items in inventories distributed against the quantities of regionalized orders and customer profiles segmented by income class that would have been impossible with previous generations of database managers.

But this beautiful setting brought with it a new problem. How to store this growing volume of data? Storage was increasingly expensive and processing was increasingly slower. As a consequence, there was the difficulty of assessing whether all this infrastructure had real value for companies.

Despite the weaknesses of the entity-relationship model, it has consolidated itself as the data management standard for transactional systems based on highly structured data.

However, the problem of processing managerial and strategic information increased every day. The growth in the volume of data that companies had to process reached an unchecked level by the end of the 1990s.

It was then that William H. Inmon (Inmon, 1992, 1996) presented his definition of DW that provided a solution characterized by:

- Subject-Oriented Guidance. DW's data structure modeling orientation is oriented towards the company's key issues, while transactional systems are focused on transactional processes and applications.

- Integration. All data created in the DW environment is created in subject segments, the data marts[8], which are integrated forming a base in which all data is integrated. Integration is made possible by adopting the following guidelines:

- o Attribute names are standardized.

- o Attribute comments are thought of according to the company as a whole and not to a specific information system.

- o The information is coded according to standards adopted by all the company's information systems.

- o The types, sizes and formats of attributes are standardized and adopted in all the company's databases

- Variance in time. While in transactional systems databases maintain data according to the processes in which they are used, in DW the timeline of the data is maintained without interruption, as its main objective is to analyze the behavior of the data over a longer period.

- Non-volatile. In DW there are only two operations: the data load and the data queries. In this structure, the data is periodically copied from the transactional database. No change or deletion allowing to derive the multidimensional data model.

---

[8] Data Mart - It is a small data warehouse, covering a certain subject area and offering more detailed information about the market (or department) in question. A set of data marts from a company make up the data warehouse.

For a better understanding of this approach, let's take the example of a cruise liner company. Using a DW, information can be obtained based on the historical series of ship voyages. It is possible to identify in which region of the world there is the highest demand for a particular cruise at a certain time of the year (Kimball et al., 2013). The detail of this query can also be expanded by identifying the origin of these passengers.

With this information in a timely manner, that is, at the end of the cruise season, it is possible for managers to plan the cruise calendar for the next season, offering advantages to passengers in a certain region of the world.

The same example applies to social programs in which it is possible for public managers to base their actions according to the historical analysis of a given subject. For example, with the data on public school enrollments, it would be possible, through the analysis of the historical series of student results, to identify in which region there are higher school dropouts and to act on the maintenance of students in the classrooms.

Improvements in virtualization technologies and improvements in hardware scalability have brought many benefits and expanded the fields of action for database managers and data warehouses. In parallel, the expansion of the performance of data marts was another factor in the expansion of the use of Data Warehouses.

Data marts had their use expanded by focusing on specific problems of the company's business, serving quick queries, behaving as small DWs that, as they were approved for use, were incorporated into the corporate DW.

The DW + data mart suite solved many managerial and strategic data generation problems, but proved inadequate to address problems that needed to process unstructured or semi-structured data.

One of the reasons for this inadequacy to the new processing demands is precisely one of the pillars of the Data Warehouse. Its structure is based on periodic loads that meet well the initial proposal of generating data for planning, financial reports and traditional marketing campaigns, but it is too slow for companies and consumers who need real-time analysis and results.

It should be noted here that unstructured content cannot be treated in conventional attributes in relational databases. As a solution to store them in databases, so that they would not be lost, the unstructured data were stored contiguous blocks of data, in fields such as BLOBs – *Binary Large Object*. This type of field was created for the storage of any type of information in binary format, within a table of a relational database.

Although very useful for storing unstructured data, this type of field does not allow its content to be used in processing because it was not possible to know what was inside them. The BLOB was widely used, then, for image storage.

In the current scenario, in which most of the data available in the world is unstructured, there is a new market, with disconnected solutions that have evolved into unified business process management platforms.

This new solution platform incorporated metadata such as information about the company's performance and characteristics of the stored information about this performance.

At the same time, requirements engineering has faced a new generation of specifications that is based on the convergence of the web with virtualization, cloud computing, and big data.

These new requirements reflect the demands of companies that are beginning to incorporate into their work process the need to manage a new generation of data sources with unprecedented quantities and varieties that need to be processed and generate useful results at a speed never seen before.

The evolution of data managers then arrives at the current technological proposal, Big Data. And there we have an issue that is very present in the analysis of companies. Is Big Data really something new in the world of data processing or is it a natural evolution of technology?

Although it seems incoherent to say that it is the result of the natural evolution of data management and something entirely new, this is the answer (Helbing, 2015a). While it builds on everything that has previously existed in data management, it introduces fundamental innovations by solving problems such as the cost of compute cycles, the increasing complexity of storage, and the management of massive databases.

Big Data makes it possible to virtualize data so that it can be stored more efficiently and more cost-effectively by utilizing cloud-based storage.

In parallel, the new data processing landscape has at its disposal improvements in the speed and reliability of networks, changes in prices and the sophistication of computer memory.

And, finally, after so many evolutions, today there is the possibility of structuring solutions, inconceivable until recently, in which companies have the potential to make intelligent use of large masses of unstructured data.

As an example of processing these large volumes of data, we have cases in which there are already companies processing petabytes of data, equivalent to 35 million files full of folders with text files or many years of HDTV content, with exceptional performance, to identify patterns of consumer behavior or find anomalies in e-commerce processes.

The adoption of Big Data does not only imply changes in companies, but also in academic and scientific segments, in research institutes and government companies.

It is important to highlight that we are still in the early stages in relation to the processing of large volumes of data as a basis for planning and anticipating changes in the market and in customer behavior.

From everything that has been exposed so far, you must have already concluded that Big Data is not just a tool, nor is it just a consequence of the evolution of database managers, but a convergence of several factors, technologies, consumers, computers in the context of the Internet.

And then we come to the concept of **Big Data** that we will adopt in this book:

Set of technologies to manage a huge volume of structured and unstructured data, at high speed, producing expected results in the expected time to enable real-time analysis and planning.

There are those who think that Big Data is just another novelty, but when we talk about Big Data, we are talking about technological innovations, new computational theories and new database managers.

The Big Data approach incorporates many different approaches to analysis to address a specific problem. Some analytics will be based on a traditional DW, while others use advanced predictive analytics.

Managing Big Data in a comprehensive, multidisciplinary and holistic way requires many different approaches so that it is possible to succeed in the company's business and in the planning of future strategies.

After performing indexing, structuring and cleaning processes of huge amounts of data, an interesting alternative to facilitate the analysis of these data is to organize subsets, according to identified patterns or certain parameters, and make them accessible to the company's professionals.

One way to implement this accessibility to data is to implement structured Data Warehouses in data marts oriented to the company's business. This approach offers compression, multi-level partitioning, and high processing parallelism.

2.4   Characteristic of Big Data analysis.

The fact that the company has at its disposal the ability to manage and analyze petabytes, soon to be exabytes, of data creates a scenario of informational reality.

With so many variables in the Big Data context, analytics can become extremely complex. A very useful analysis in the fight against fraud, for example, uses predictive models that combine structured and unstructured data.

In the traditional approach to analytical and strategic reporting, the company expects data to be the matrix for answering questions about what to do and when to do it. Data is usually integrated as fields in general-purpose business applications. In the Big Data approach, software companies are developing specialized applications in the unstructured and multiple architecture of Big Data.

The best examples of these apps focus on areas such as healthcare, education, manufacturing, traffic management, and e-commerce. A common feature of all these Big Data applications is that they are prepared to process large volumes, at high speeds and receiving a wide variety of data.

In healthcare, a Big Data application may be able to monitor intensive care units to identify when a patient will need some more serious support. In a factory, a Big Data application can be used to prevent a machine from interrupting the production process. A Big Data air traffic management application can reduce congestion and the risk of accidents at busy airports.

2.5   The old meets the new: distributed computing.

Distributed computing has been used for more than 50 years. Initially, the technology was the basis of computer science research as a way to reduce the burden of computing tasks and attack complex problems without the cost of large computing systems.

Distributed computing is a technique that allows individual computers to be networked together as if they were a single environment.

One of the first successful ventures into distributed computing was a project funded by the U.S. Defense Advanced Research Projects Agency, DARPA.[9]

The result of the research gave rise to the development of the Internet. Initially, it was designed to create an interconnection network system that would support non-commercial research in collaboration between scientists. In the early days of the Internet, these computers used to be connected by telephone lines

---

[9] Defense Advanced Research Projects Agency – DARPA. The Defense Advanced Research Projects Agency, created in February 1958, initially as ARPA, by U.S. military personnel and researchers under the supervision of President Eisenhower, as a reaction of the United States to the technological victory of the then Soviet Union with the launch of the first artificial satellite, Sputnik 1, with the original objective of maintaining the technological superiority of the U.S. and warning against possible technological advances by potential adversaries.

As the technology matured, common protocols like TCP[10] helped proliferate the technology and the network. When IP[11] was added, the project changed from a closed network for a collection of scientists to a potentially commercial platform for transferring email around the world.

Throughout the 1980s, new Internet-based services began to emerge on the market as a commercial alternative to the DARPA network. In 1992, the U.S. Congress passed the Advanced and Scientific Technology Act which, for the first time, allowed commercial use of this powerful networking technology.

With its continued explosive growth, the Internet has established itself as a global distributed network and remains the best example of the power of distributed computing.

In some network topologies, individual computing entities simply pass messages to each other. In other situations, a distributed computing environment may share resources ranging from memory to networking to storage.

All distributed computing models have in common the fact that they are a group of networked computers that work together to run a workload or processing.

---

[10] Transmission Control Protocol - TCP. The Transmission Control Protocol is part of the group of communication protocols that support the activities of users on the Internet. Its function is basically to check for errors in the transmitted data.

[11] The pure internet protocol, i.e., IP, is the main communication protocol on the network. He is responsible for addressing and forwarding the packets that travel over the internet. The IP, however, does not ensure the delivery of its data packets. Therefore, it is common for this protocol to be combined with TCP.

There were hundreds of companies creating a software infrastructure intended to provide a common platform to support a highly distributed computing environment before the Internet became a commercial network.

However, each vendor or standards company developed its own RPCs[12] that all customers, commercial software developers, and partners would have to adopt and support.

RPC is a primitive mechanism used to send work to a remote computer, and it usually requires waiting for remote work to complete before other work can continue. With vendors implementing proprietary RPCs, it became impractical to imagine that any one company would be able to create a universal standard for distributed computing.

By the mid-1990s, Internet protocols had replaced these primitive approaches and became the basis for what distributed computing is today.

2.6   Distributed computing.

Computing resources can be distributed in a variety of ways. The consequence is the need to have several models of distributed computing. For example, you can distribute a set of programs on the same physical server and use messaging services to enable them to communicate and transmit information. It is also possible to have several different systems or servers, each with its own memory, that can work together to solve a problem.

---

[12] Remote Procedure Call - RPC.   Remote Procedure Call is a cross-process communication technology that allows a computer program to call a procedure in another address space, usually on another computer, connected by a network.

It's important to note that not all problems require distributed computing. If there is no major time constraint, complex processing can be done remotely through a specialized service.

Previously, when companies needed to do complex data analysis, they were moved to an external service or entity where many additional resources were available for processing.

In this situation, the issue was not that companies did not mind waiting to get the results they needed. The situation was imposed because it was not economically feasible to purchase enough computing equipment to handle these emerging requirements.

In many situations, due to costs, companies worked only with portions of data, rather than trying to capture all of it. The analysts wanted all the data, but they had to try to work with small chunks in an attempt to capture the data needed for the problem at hand. The ability to leverage distributed computing and parallel processing techniques has greatly transformed the landscape and dramatically reduced latency.

There are special cases, such as HFT[13], where low latency can only be achieved by physically locating the servers in a single location.

2.7   The problem with latency.

One of the most pressing problems for success in data management, especially when dealing with large amounts of data, is latency.

Latency is the delay in executing a task. Latency is an issue in all aspects of computing, including communications, data management, system performance, and more.

---

[13] High Frequency Trading – HFT. High Frequency Trading is a concept associated with algorithmic trading and refers to the use of powerful algorithms, which allow you to trade financial assets automatically with maximum speed. It is a way of using technology, the "robots", to make very short-term investments, lasting seconds.

Distributed computing and parallel processing techniques can make a significant difference in the latency experienced by customers, suppliers, and partners.

Most Big Data applications are dependent on low latency due to Big Data's requirements for data speed, volume, and variety. It is not possible to develop a big data application in a high-latency environment. The need to check data in near real-time is also greatly affected by latency.

The consolidation of the Internet as a platform for all uses, from commerce to medicine, has given rise to the demand for a new generation of data management.

By the late 1990s, companies like Google, Yahoo!, and Amazon were able to expand their business models by leveraging cheap hardware for compute and storage.

However, a few years later, these companies were already in need of a new generation of software technologies that would allow them to monetize the huge amounts of data they were capturing from customers without waiting for the results of analytical processing.

One of the factors that powers *cloud computing*[14], then, is the continuous and growing need to process disparate data. The cloud model allows for large-scale and distributed operation.

The definition of the architecture should be based on what your company wants to do with its structured and unstructured data. This also determines the need to understand the input data structures to put that data in the right place.

---

[14] Cloud Computing. Cloud Computing is the offering of on-demand computing services through the internet. These services include file storage, networks, software, databases, servers, and many others. The main feature is that system makes it unnecessary to save files and install programs on your own computer.

A noteworthy aspect in the Big Data universe is the fact that, many times, the company does not need to own all the data it will use. Many examples demonstrate this situation.

You may be using data from social media, data from third-party e-commerce measurements, or even data from satellites. Much of this data may have been previously siloed and it is not a prerequisite that it reaches your company in real time.

Our focus is on the situation where the company needs to process large volumes of data, at high speeds, and they are varied in nature. The problem is that you can't get business value from dealing with a variety of disconnected data sources.

The components that become necessary are connectors and metadata:

- Connectors. Your analytics may need some connectors that allow you to pull data from multiple big data sources. You may need a Twitter or Facebook connector. Or you may need to integrate a data warehouse with a big data source that's off-site so you can analyze the data sources together.

- Metadata. Metadata is the definitions, mappings, and other characteristics used to describe how to find, access, and use a company's data components (and software).

An example of metadata is data about an account number. This can include the number, description, data type, name, address, phone number, and privacy level.

Metadata can be used to organize your company's data stores and handle new and changing data sources. They are critical components for the integration of data with different structures.

While the concept of metadata is not new, it is changing and evolving in the context of Big Data. In the traditional world of metadata, it's

important to have a catalog that provides a single view of all data sources. But to control different sources and types of data, this catalog can no longer be limited to a single view. It will need to handle different metadata for each type of data. You may even need to use an analytics tool to help you understand the underlying metadata.

3 Four Steps to a Successful Project.

Different companies in different industries need to manage their data differently. But some common business issues are why Big Data is considered as a way to plan and execute business strategies.

Hence, we have a very current question:

– What does the company hope to achieve with the use of Big Data?

This is not an easy question to answer. The biggest challenge for the company is to be able to look into the future and anticipate what might change and why.

Companies want to be able to make good decisions faster and more efficiently. The company wants to apply this knowledge to adopt measures that can change business outcomes.

Leaders also need to understand the nuances of the impacts of their business decisions across all product lines and their partner ecosystem. The best companies take a holistic approach to data.

Four steps are part of the planning process that applies to Big Data: plan, analyze, verify, and act.

The following sections describe what these steps mean.

3.1 Step 1: Plan with data.

With the amount of data available to businesses, there are dangers in making assumptions based on a single view of it. The only way to be sure that leaders are relying on a balanced perspective with all the elements to make good decisions is to have a clear understanding of how this source data is related.

But in general, companies have only a small amount of the data that would be needed for these decisions. Thus, the company needs to adopt a planning track to determine what data is needed to plan new strategies and new directions.

For example, if a company needs to expand the type of services it can offer to existing customers, it will need to conduct data-driven analysis of what customers are buying and how it is changing.

Questions arise, such as:

- What do customers like and dislike about products?

- What are competitors offering?

- What new macro trends are emerging that will affect customer preferences?

- How are your customers reacting to your products and those of your competitors?

It's easy to see that if you can find effective ways to manage data, your company will have a powerful planning tool. Even if the data can confirm the existing strategy, it can indicate unexpected new directions.

Part of the planning process requires using a variety of data to test assumptions and think about the business differently.

3.2   Step 2: Analyze, analyze, and analyze.

After step 1 where the company has understood its business objectives, it's time to start analyzing the data itself as part of the planning process. This is not an independent process.

Performing in Big Data analytics requires learning a set of new tools and new skills. Many companies will need to hire some Big Data scientists to be able to understand how to turn this huge amount of data from a problem into a business opportunity.

The Big Data analytics market is very immature, so it's still hard to find highly abstract and easy-to-use tools to support analytics. Big data analytics is a dynamic area that is undergoing very rapid change.

3.3 Step 3: Check the results.

One thing that often happens in the first moments of Big Data deployment in companies is to validate the results, but forget to do a reality check. Reality analysis implies verifying that the data is useful and applies to the reality of the company's business.

To do so, it is necessary to have sensible and sufficient answers to questions like these:

- Does the analysis reflect the expected results for the business?

- Is the data used accurate enough, or do they have additional problems to be solved?

- Do data sources have real potential to increase the company's business planning?

This is the time to make sure your business is relying on data from sources that will lead the business in the right direction. Many companies use third-party data sources and may not have the time to sufficiently check the quality of the data.

Be aware of this issue. When you're planning and making business decisions based on analytics, you need to make sure you have a strong foundation.

3.4 Step 4: Acting in the right direction.

After this cycle of analysis is complete, it's time to put the plan into action, but actions should be part of an overall planning cycle that repeats itself, especially as markets become more dynamic.

Each time a company starts a new strategy, it is critical to create a constant cycle of Big Data business evaluation.

The approach of acting on the results of the Big Data analysis and then testing the results of the execution of the business strategy is the key to success. Big Data adds the critical element of being able to leverage real results to verify that the strategy is working as intended.

Sometimes the results of a new strategy may not match the expectations of the company's managers. In some cases, this will mean redefining the strategy and in other situations, the unintended consequences will lead the company in a new direction that may end up having a better result.

3.5   Some advantages of Big Data.

Using technology intelligently can make your company secure its space in the market, standing out from competitors and even becoming a leader in the segment. And knowing some examples of Big Data applications can make you realize the secrets to business success.

Big Data works as a compass for administrators to make the right decision about the direction their company should take. It increases efficiency and speeds up the development of companies of any industry and size.

3.5.1   Examples of Big Data applications in HR.

The purpose of Big Data in the human resources sector is to replace assumptions with certainties, maximizing the success rate in hiring.

Although this department is quite subjective, cutting-edge computers process a wide variety of information much more accurately than humans.

Big Data can guarantee the following benefits:

01. Reduce bad hires.

Even with the support of the best professionals in the area, it is possible that employees who do not fit the company's profile will be hired. As a result, there are losses in this hiring, as there was capital expenditure in interviews, training, loss of productivity, etc.

Using Big Data technology, it is possible to quickly analyze all candidate data, including whether their ideologies and goals are in line with the company's principles, resulting in an increase in the probability of hiring the ideal employee.

02. Increase the retention rate.

After hiring the ideal employee, HR's goal is to keep him in the company, after all, it is the employees who move the company internally, they provide the service or produce the product. The Big Data algorithm constantly studies the history, performance, and satisfaction of each employee.

It is possible to identify precisely if they are satisfied at work, what the existing problems are, and the means to solve them. By doing so, their productivity will be enhanced both by their satisfaction and by the elimination of obstacles to their tasks.

03. Predict performance.

With Big Data, it is possible to predict whether a certain employee will be able to stand out from others in the sector, whether they have innovative ideas for the business or talent for other activities in the company. For this, a thorough and constant analysis is necessary. Predilections include:

- Speed of learning;

- Effective in the company;

- Commitment to work; and

- Idleness and probability of occupational accidents occurring.

Electronically aggregated data is automatically updated and analyzed in real time. By pairing them with performance from past jobs, it will allow an anticipation of their future performance.

3.5.2   In retail stores.

The biggest challenge for retailers is to predict the behavior and preferences of their clientele, whether new or existing. After all, consumer tastes are constantly changing with the emergence of new fashions and trends.

But this obstacle can be easily solved with the adoption of Big Data.

01. Generate recommendations.

Big Data uses the customer's purchase history and searches on the Internet to generate a list of products that may also be of interest. With this system, your company will be able to attract the attention of even new customers, as the catalog will be based on the general search on the Internet and not only on your website.

This increases the time consumers spend on your website, the chances of purchases, and the popularity of your business across the board.

02. Know your clientele.

The technology is interconnected to social networks and performs intelligent searches on keywords, trends and accesses to other pages. With this, you can identify which products attract each type of customer, those that are part of only one niche, and which are widely popular, maximizing sales of all products on the site.

03. Make strategic decisions.

Usually, common apps inform the number of products sold, so it is possible to know which are the most popular and generate the most revenue.

However, Big Data goes further by demonstrating which products are gaining or losing popularity and comparing prices with competitors among other indicators. All this contributes to the administrator devising more effective strategies, including in physical retail.

3.5.3   In the area of health.

The health sectors constantly work with urgencies and emergencies and these events generate disorder in any company, causing certain environments to suffer from a lack of employees while others have a certain slowness.

For this reason, it is essential to have the help of a computer to control the time and number of employees in each area of the establishment, maximizing productivity and satisfying customers.

01. Create electronic files.

Electronic Health Records –EHRs, the electronic health record is a record of the patient's entire history of diseases, allergies, tests, and lab results. This saves time and money with repeat tests or interviews with the individual.

02. Receive real-time alerts.

It is possible that this function is in the cloud, that is, the alert will take place in any location, and it is not necessary for the user to be near a computer terminal to receive it.

In this way, Big Data also emerges as a fundamental tool for preserving health in general by creating real-time alerts. For example, if the patient's blood pressure increases significantly, alerts will automatically be sent to the doctor to take action.

03. Predict needs.

Patients with complex hospital histories or who suffer from multiple conditions require special attention, taking up a lot of doctors' time.

Big Data can assist in the execution of an instant study of your condition, anticipating needs and assisting doctors in their preparations.

Health entities, through analytical algorithms, can build and analyze patterns in medical care, either through structured or unstructured data. Big Data has been useful in supporting medical decision-making, as well as in predictability and tracking.

In the USA, the Texas Health Harris Methodist Hospital Alliance has analyzed the information from medical sensors in order to predict the evolution of its patients, as well as to monitor the patients' movements throughout the hospitalization period.

In this way, the hospital can obtain reports, alerts, key performance indicators and interactive visualizations resulting from predictive analysis. This analysis allows the hospital to offer the appropriate services and with greater efficiency, thus improving existing operations, as well as its ability to prevent possible medical risks.

Another example is related to the work that has been developed by some researchers from the Universities of Heidelberg and Stanford who have built a system that aims to detect diseases using the visual diagnosis of images that according to taxonomy are called natural.

Natural images consist of images such as skin lesions, for example, to help determine if they are cancerous. According to the study's leaders, the system's predictive ability performed better when compared to professional dermatologists.

On the one hand, the general population would benefit, in the sense that the earlier a disease is diagnosed, the better the chances of treatment. On the other hand, the state would also benefit as it could reduce its costs related to the treatment of advanced diseases.

3.5.4   Environment.

Due to the great advances of modern society, the environment is often forced to pay the price for human progress. Big data is enabling companies like Rainforest Connection, a U.S. nonprofit, to use artificial intelligence tools, such as Google's TensorFlow, in natural resource conservation programs around the world.

Its platform can detect illegal activities, such as logging, in areas where forests are most unprotected or most susceptible to such action. These activities can be recorded only thanks to the analysis of information from audio sensors that allow auscultation in real time or almost real to several forests.

3.5.5   Assistance in crisis management.

The crises in question range from natural or man-made disasters to search and rescue missions to crises related to the emergence of diseases. With regard to crisis management assistance, examples emerge, such as the use of AI combined with information originating from satellites that have made it possible to map and predict the progression of forest fires.

In this way, these new instruments have allowed the intervention of firefighters to be more precise and more effective. The possible use of drones, once again associated with AI, to rescue missing people in wilderness areas has also been explored.

3.5.6   For small businesses.

Big Data should not be ignored by any company, not even small ones. It is common to think that a new business does not need Big Data to process information, but this is a serious mistake.

01. Make better use of social networks.

Big Data identifies mentions made to the company on social networks whose communication platforms include Twitter, Facebook, Instagram, Snapchat and others that allow the exchange of public messages.

Technology will differentiate the posts of positive or negative experiences, allowing you to get to know customers better, find more effective ways to win them over and sell the company's product to them.

02. Get to know consumers better.

It is possible to collect data from users' experience with your products through the devices they are using, such as laptops, desktop computers, smartphones, among others.

By knowing their problems and tastes, it is possible to know how the company's products and services should be updated to better please consumers and build their loyalty.

03. Create better marketing.

Maintaining a constant analysis of information about your customers, such as age, gender, ethnicity, among other elements, will allow the creation of

4   Myths and Trends.

With the increasing popularity of Big Data, there are many misconceptions about it. It is necessary to be aware of the true potential of Big Data and in which situations it should be applied.

Big data embeds significant changes in the way we think about data treatment and analysis. Treating very large volumes changes our perception of how to look at data. In practice, when we change scale, our perception changes.

For example, if we leave our world where we recognize the difference between a solid object and the air around us and fall into another scale, such as the quantum level, everything becomes an atom. The differences between objects and air, as we know it in our daily lives, cease to exist. The same happens when we go from a small volume to a monstrous one at least, of data.

Several myths around Big Data have emerged. And, if you focus too much on them, the overall efficiency of the business can suffer.

4.1.1   Myths focused on Big Data.

Some of the most well-known myths are discussed below.

1.   Big Data is just Hype.

It is a very popular opinion of the masses that Big Data is exaggerated. They believe that the sheer volume of data is nothing but the "same old data," just in enormous quantities.

It is believed that there is nothing new in the concept, except that only data scientists can read the information from the data. This and the additional costs included in the technology make it even more expensive.

Thus, there is an expectation that Big Data will not be used by smaller companies for a few years.

2. There are no problems that cannot be solved with Big Data.

    Companies believe that any problem related to analytics is a big data problem, but not everything is a big data problem.

    For example, if your company is trying to combine a few terabytes of information with a few fields according to some conditions, that's really not a big data problem.

3. Big Data can anticipate what the future will look like.

    This is not completely a myth, but it is what some would call a half-truth. The correct use of Big Data can indeed provide some information for predicting the future, but this information is based on historical data. This means that the insights will depend on the data that has been analyzed and the user's requirements or questions.

    Therefore, Big Data is not 100% reliable for future predictions.

4. Big Data is only applicable in large companies.

    Many believe that Big Data is only for large companies with big budgets. This is one of the reasons why only large companies use Big Data solutions.

    Big Data requires a lot of capital for technological installation and manpower. However, as the cost of these components decreases, the power of these technologies will also increase, and more startups will be able to use these technologies.

    At the same time, we must remember that cloud computing is also making these technologies and platforms available to smaller businesses at a lower cost.

    Therefore, Big Data is becoming accessible to all types of businesses.

5. Big Data is better, less organized.

    In Big Data, the accuracy of the information, among other factors, depends on the magnitude and reliability of the data being analyzed. Therefore, this means that whether the data is structured, unstructured, organized or unorganized, there is no connection between this and the results obtained.

    Large amounts of incorrect data can also lead to poor decisions. Another example of this is data confusion, as Big Data analysis is not a very easy job. However, as analytics solutions are becoming more and more user-friendly, it will be easier to analyze the data.

    Therefore, the challenge is to clean up this messy data and analyze it to get proper data.

6. Big Data technologies will not mature.

    Today, Big Data technologies are simply a network of different types of software with special capabilities for analyzing large volumes of data, and they are expected to evolve over time.

    Thus, Big Data technology is not fully mature, as there are many flaws in these network components and in their ecosystem. Big Data will gradually evolve as more and more people start to adopt it.

7. Big Data will replace existing Data Warehouses.

    This is a really dangerous myth. Big Data technology is not yet developed enough to meet the needs of all kinds of data-related problems. In addition, Big Data technologies and platforms do not replace traditional Data Warehouses or RDBMS.

    Big Data is for specific requirements and should not be applied in any situation. Thus, Big Data is not intended to replace current Data

Warehouses, although it may meet some requirements of Data Warehouses in the near future.

Big Data strategy is a responsibility of the IT team alone.

Having an IT department in a company really helps, as it is the one that sets up the various types of software and hardware needed for Big Data.

However, a dedicated IT team alone is not enough to deploy a big data strategy. The Big Data strategy helps to make better decisions, but for this to be an advantage, the decision-making department must carefully evaluate the solutions.

8. Hadoop is the best solution for Big Data.

   Hadoop is often considered the best Big Data solution. However, there are many alternatives to Hadoop. The best solution really depends on your own requirements.

9. The term "Big Data" is new, and the data available today is also very new.

   The concept of Big Data and its uses are actually very old. Many companies used Big Data before it was officially called "Big Data," so this myth isn't entirely true.

Are these myths really important?

These Big Data myths are very obstructive and can result in poor business decisions. They can contribute to the company wasting resources that could be better used to increase its market share.

Therefore, knowing the full truth makes a difference, as half-truths can be really dangerous for business.

4.1.2   The best trends for 2030.

A recent study published by MicroStrategy points out the digital transformation and data analytics trends that are coming with everything by 2030.

1. Deep Learning.

    For Frank J. Bernhard, chief data officer at SHAPE-Digital Strategy, deep learning has already moved from the trend stage to a consolidation status. And what does this mean?

    It is no longer something new, and its implementation is almost mandatory. The difference lies in how each company employs the practice in its operations, and what strategies they are taking to stand out compared to the competition.

2. Semantic Graphics.

    Roxane Edjlali, senior director of product management at MicroStrategy and a former Gartner analyst, says that semantic graphs are essential to adding value to the business: "The semantic graph will become the backbone that supports data and analytics in an ever-changing data landscape. Companies that don't use a semantic graph risk seeing analytics-related ROI[15] drop due to increasing complexity and the resulting organizational costs."

3. Human vision.

---

[15] Return on Investment – ROI. Return on Investment is a metric used to know how much the company has earned from investments, especially in the Marketing area. To calculate ROI, you need to raise the total revenue, subtract the costs from it, and divide that result by the costs as well.

Data is excellent, but for Chandana Gopal, Research Director at IDC, the people who apply it also need to be familiar with ethnographic issues and the human context behind all the situations collected. According to Gopal, the data, in a crude form, are incomplete if they do not involve this amount.

4. Automated Machine Learning.

Automated Machine Learning, or AutoML, is the bet of Marcus Borba, founder and consultant at Borba Consulting. For him, the rapid evolution of machine learning services in recent years has enabled the emergence of even more agile and automated functions in this sector, being of great value to brands, mainly due to their ease of use and independence.

5. Embeeded Analytics.

According to Doug Henschen, VP and analyst at Constellation Research, the new generation of Embedded Analytics will accelerate time to time to gain important data.

"Concise analysis delivered in the context of specific applications and interfaces accelerates decision-making. This style of embedding and curating concise, contextual analytics can take longer, and with advancements including no-code and low-code development methods, we're seeing increasing adoption of the next generation of Embedded Analytics."

6. Data and Analytics.

In the same way that human vision is necessary to complement data intelligence, companies need to get used to diversifying these reference bases.

7. David Menninger.

Vice president and director of Ventana Research, explains that large companies hardly have an exclusive and standardized Data and Analytics platform, and this trend of varying sources will be increasingly common.

8. Data-driven skills.

MicroStrategy's vice president of education, Hugh Owen, explains that data-driven skills will become a requirement in companies, which should start not only recruiting more people with analytical skills, but training current employees for these skills.

9. Artificial intelligence.

Just as Deep and Machine Learning have already become mandatory in a data-oriented market, artificial intelligence is also an arm that cannot be left out in business strategies.

Forrester Research's team of researchers indicates that by 2028, data science teams will be spending 70% to 90% of their time building new and better AI models to be deployed.

10. Mobile Intelligence.

Mark Smith, CEO and research director at Ventana Research, suggests that this year we will see half of companies reevaluating their mobile operations and realizing that they are insufficient to meet customer expectations. After that, a major remodeling of these digital functions will be observed.

11. Experience Management.

R "Ray" Wang, founder and principal analyst at Constellation Research, comments that AI will power Experience Management: "As applications are broken down by the business process to headless microservices, automation and intelligence will play an important role in creating personalization and efficiency at mass, and at scale. The Intelligent Enterprise will bring context and data analytics to drive its next actions."

5   HADOOP.

Hadoop is one of the terms that are part of the vocabulary of emerging technologies. And it deserves the prominence it has been receiving. It can be described as a set of *open source*[16] programs and procedures that serve as the framework for data operations.

Due to its importance in today's Big Data architecture, Hadoop has been given an entire chapter in this book so that it is very detailed.

Although recent, Hadoop[17] has stood out as an effective tool, being used by large corporations such as IBM, Oracle, Facebook, Yahoo!, among others.

But to get to this point, some important events have occurred in recent years, as the following historical facts demonstrate:

- February 2003: Jeffrey Dean and Sanjay Ghemawat, two Google engineers, develop MapReduce technology, which makes it possible to optimize the indexing and cataloging of data about Web pages and their links. MapReduce allows you to break down a big problem into several pieces and distribute them on several computers. This technique made Google's search system faster even though it ran on conventional and less reliable computers, thus reducing costs related to infrastructure;

- October 2003: Google develops the Google File System, a distributed file system GoogleFS (later called GFS), designed to support the storage and processing of large volumes of data

---

[16] Available at no cost for everyone to use and modify.

[17] http://hadoop.apache.org.

from MapReduce technology;

- December 2004: Google publishes the article *Simplified Data Processing on Large Clusters*, authored by engineers Dean and Ghemawat, where they present the main concepts and characteristics of the MapReduce technology, but without details about the implementation;

- December 2005: Software consultant Douglas Cutting announced the implementation of a version of MapReduce and the distributed file system based on GFS and MapReduce articles published by Google engineers. The implementation is part of the Nutch subproject, adopted by the open source community to create a web search engine, commonly called a *web crawler* (a software that automates the indexing of pages) and a parser document format *parser*. Later Nutch would be hosted as the Lucene project, at the Apache Software Foundation, with the main function of providing a powerful search and indexing engine for documents stored in various formats, such as text files, web pages, spreadsheets, or any other format from which textual information can be extracted;

- February 2006: Yahoo! decides to hire Cutting and invest in the Nutch project, keeping the source open. That same year, the project is named Hadoop, becoming an independent project of the Apache Software Foundation;

- April 2007: Yahoo! announces that it has successfully run a Hadoop application on a cluster of 1,000 machines. Also on that date, Yahoo! becomes the largest sponsor of the project. A few years later, the company already had more than 40,000 machines running Hadoop (White, 2010);

- January 2008: Apache Hadoop, version 0.15.2, matures as an incubated project at the Apache Foundation, and becomes one of the company's main open projects.

- July 2008: A Hadoop application in one of Yahoo!'s clusters breaks the world record for processing speed in sorting 1 terabyte of data. The cluster was composed of 910 machines and performed the sorting in 209 seconds, surpassing the previous record of 297 seconds;

- September 2009: Big Data company Cloudera hires Cutting as project leader. Cloudera is a company that redistributes a commercial version derived from Apache Hadoop;

- December 2011: Six years after its release, Apache Hadoop makes its stable version (1.0.0) available. Among the improvements, the use of the Kerberos network authentication protocol, for greater network security; the incorporation of the HBase subproject, supporting BigTable; and support for the WebHDFS interface, which allows HTTP access for reading and writing data;

- May 2012: Apache releases Hadoop version 2.0, including high availability in the file system (HDFS) and code improvements.

Being hosted as an Apache Software Foundation project, Hadoop follows Apache's licensing model, which is much more flexible than other free software licensing modalities, allowing modifications and redistribution of source code. In this way, several companies have emerged in the market distributing Hadoop implementations.

Hadoop is designed to:

- It processes large amounts of structured and unstructured data, terabytes to petabytes, and is deployed on commodity racks servers as a Hadoop cluster.

- Parallelize data processing in compute on nodes to speed up calculations and hide latency. At its core, Hadoop has two primary components:

    - Hadoop distributed file system. A reliable system with high bandwidth and low-cost data storage clustering that makes it easy to manage related files across multiple machines

    - MapReduce Engine: A high-performance parallel/distributed data processing processing implementations of the MapReduce algorithm.

The flexible nature of a Hadoop system allows businesses to be able to add or modify their data system as their needs change, using inexpensive and readily available parts from any IT vendor.

Servers can be added or removed from the cluster dynamically because Hadoop is designed to be "self-healing." In other words, Hadoop is able to detect changes, including failures, and adjust to those changes and continue to operate without interruption.

The support and enthusiasm of the open source community behind it has led to great strides towards making Big Data analytics more accessible for everyone.

In its raw state, using the basic modules provided by Apache, Hadoop can be very complex, even for IT professionals. That's why several commercial versions have been developed, such as Cloudera[18], which simplifies the task of installing and running a Hadoop system, as well as offering training and support services.

Currently, Hadoop is the most widely used system for providing hardware data storage and processing. Almost every major company in the Internet world uses it, and since it's a free platform, modifications made to the software by expert engineers at Amazon and Google, for example, are fed back into the development community, where they're often used to improve the "official" product.

This form of collaborative development between volunteer and commercial users is a key feature of open source software.

5.1   What is the relationship between Hadoop and Big Data?

Hadoop is used to process big data workloads because it is highly scalable. To increase the processing power of your Hadoop cluster, you can add more servers with the CPU and memory resources needed to meet your needs.

Hadoop provides a high level of durability and availability, while continuing to process computational analytical workloads in parallel. The combination of availability, durability, and processing scalability makes Hadoop an ideal choice for data-intensive workloads.

Some advantages of Hadoop are:

- Increased speed and agility.

- Reduced administrative complexity.

---

[18] https://www.cloudera.com/. Cloudera's platform uses analytics and machine learning to generate data insights through a secure connection. Cloudera's platform works across hybrid, multi-cloud, and on-premises architectures and provides cross-functional analytics across the entire AI data lifecycle.

- Integration with other cloud services.

- Improved availability and disaster recovery.

- Flexible capacity.

While the advantages outweigh the disadvantages, Hadoop also has problems. Because the data is stored in blocks, query tasks will have to fetch all the blocks to mount the file, making access to the data problematic.

Some analytical algorithms may also not perform properly in Hadoop, as they may require the use of specific CPU instructions.

Security is another critical point in Hadoop, which has been gaining more and more attention from the framework's developers. Ideally, you should implement the Kerberos protocol[19] to perform basic security processes within the clusters.

5.2   Hadoop architecture.

Hadoop provides an architecture for MapReduce applications to work in a distributed manner on a cluster of machines, organized into one master machine and multiple slave machines.

To simplify the development of these applications, it is possible to install and run the framework in simplified mode, using only one machine (which will simulate a parallelizable/distributed environment).

Hadoop is composed of modules, each of which carries an essential task for computer systems designed for data analysis.

---

[19] Kerberos is a protocol developed to provide authentication in user/server applications. It acts as the third party in this process, offering certified authentication to the user.

A number of other procedures, libraries, or features have come to be considered part of the Hadoop framework in recent years, but the Hadoop Distributed File System, Hadoop MapReduce, Hadoop Common, and Hadoop YARN are the four main ones.

The core modules of Hadoop are:

1. Hadoop Distributed File System.

This module is one of the most important because it allows data to be stored in a simple and accessible format, among a large number of linked storage devices.

The "file system" is the method used by a computer to store data that can be found and used. Typically, this is determined by the computer's operating system, however, a Hadoop system uses its own file system that sits "above" the host computer's file system, which means it can be accessed using any computer with a compatible operating system.

2. MapReduce.

MapReduce gets its name from the two basic operations performed by the module:

1. Read data from the database, putting it into a format suitable for analysis, the map; and

2. Perform mathematical operations, for example by counting the number of men over 30 in a customer database, the reduction.

It is MapReduce that guarantees the tools to explore data in various ways.

3. Hadoop Common.

Provides the tools (in Java) needed for the user's computer systems (Windows, Unix, or any other) to read data stored in the Hadoop file system.

4. YARN[20]

The final module is YARN, which manages the resources of the systems that store the data and perform the analysis.

5.2.1   Additional components.

In addition to the core modules, there are other projects in the Apache community that add functionality to Hadoop, such as:

- Ambari. Web-based tool for the support, management and monitoring of other Hadoop modules such as HDFS, mapreduce, Hive, hcatalog, hbase, *Zookeeper,* Oozie, *Pig* and *Sqoop* .

- Avro. Data serialization system.

- Cassandra. Scalable, fault-tolerant database.

- Flume and Chukwa. Systems that handle the collection of occurrences (logs) for Hadoop monitoring.

- Hbase. Scalable, distributed database that supports structured data storage for large tables.

- Hive. DW infrastructure that provides data summarization and

---

[20] YARN - Yet Another Resource Negotiator.

ad hoc queries.

- Mahout. System for developing machine learning applications and library with data mining functions.

- Pig. provides a high-level query language (*Pig Latin*) oriented to data flow, and an execution framework for parallel computing.

- *Zookeeper.* High-performance coordination service for distributed applications.

5.3 Hadoop architecture processes.

For Hadoop to work, five processes are required: *NameNode*, *DataNode*, Secondary*NameNode*, JobTracker, and TaskTracker. The first three are part of the MapReduce programming model, and the last two are part of the HDFS file system. The *NameNode*, JobTracker, and Secondary*NameNode components* are unique to the entire application, while the *DataNode* and TaskTracker are instantiated for each machine in the cluster.

Given the two main components of Hadoop (MapReduce and HDFS), the basic architecture will be explained below.

5.3.1 Hadoop Distributed File System.

Hadoop Distributed File System (HDFS) is a versatile, resilient, and bundled approach to managing files in a big data environment. It is a distributed file system, designed to store very large files, with streaming data access pattern, using clusters of servers easily found on the market and of low or medium cost.

HDFS is not recommended for applications that need quick access to a particular record, but for applications in which it is necessary to read a very large amount of data. Another issue that should be noted is that it should not be used to read many small files, given the memory overhead involved.

Metadata is defined as "data about data." Software designers have used metadata for decades under various names, such as data dictionary, directory metadata, and more recently, *tags*[21].

The metadata in HDFS is *a template*[22] to provide a detailed description of the following data:

- When the file was created, accessed, modified, and deleted.

- Where the file blocks are stored in the *cluster*.

- Who has access authorization to view or modify the file.

- How many files are stored in the *cluster*.

- How many DataNodes are in the *cluster*.

- The location of the transaction log for the *cluster*.

The HDFS metadata is stored in the *NameNode*, and while the set is operating, all metadata is loaded into the physical memory of the *NameNodes server*.

For the best performance, the *NameNode server* should have a lot of physical memory and, ideally, a lot of solid-state disks. Regarding performance, the more, the better.

---

[21] Tags are words that serve as a label and help organize information, grouping those that have received the same tagging, making it easier to find other related ones.

[22] A template is a template to be followed, with a predefined structure that facilitates the development and creation of content from something built a priori.

HDFS has the concept of blocks, just like Unix, but its blocks are usually 64MB in size. A file that is too large can have blocks stored on more than one server. With this fixed-size block concept, it is easier to calculate storage needs.

HDFS has 2 types of Nodes:

- *NameNode* (or *Master*). Stores file distribution information and metadata.

- *DataNode* (or *Worker*). Stores the data itself.

So *NameNode* needs to always be available. To ensure availability, it is possible to have a backup, similar to *Cold Failover*, or to have a Secondary Master on another server. In this second option, in the event of a failure of the primary, the secondary can take over very quickly.

Because in Big Data processing data is written once and then read many times, instead of the constant write-reads of other data processing, HDFS is an excellent choice to support the analysis of large amounts of data.

5.3.1.1 NameNode.

Responsible for managing the data stored in HDFS, recording the information about which *DataNodes* are responsible for which data blocks of each file, organizing all this information in a metadata table.

Its functions include mapping the location, dividing the files into blocks, forwarding the blocks to the slave nodes, obtaining the metadata of the files, and controlling the location of their replicas.

As *NameNode* is constantly accessed, for performance reasons, it keeps all its information in memory. It integrates the HDFS system and is located on the application master node, together with the *jobtracker*

Data nodes aren't very smart, but *NameNode* is. Data nodes constantly ask *NameNode* if there's anything for them to do. This continuous monitoring also tells *NameNode* which nodes are stopped and what the level of overhead is for the nodes that are operational.

Data nodes also communicate with each other so that they can cooperate during normal file system operations. This is necessary because the blocks of a file are usually stored on multiple nodes.

Since the *NameNode* is so critical to the correct operation of the cluster, it can be duplicated to protect processing against a point of failure.

5.3.1.2   DataNode.

Responsible for storing the content of the files on slave computers. Because HDFS is a distributed file system, it is common to have multiple instances of *DataNode* in a hadoop application, allowing files to be partitioned into blocks and then replicated on different machines.

A *DataNode* can store multiple blocks, including different files, however, they need to constantly report to *NameNode*, informing it about the operations being performed on the blocks.

DataNodes are not intelligent, but they are resilient. Within the HDFS cluster, blocks of data are replicated across multiple data nodes, and access is managed by NameNode. The replication engine is designed for optimal efficiency when all nodes in the *cluster* are collected in a *rack*.

In fact, *NameNode* uses a "rack ID" to track the data nodes in the *cluster. HDFS clusters are sometimes referred to as "rack clients." Data nodes also provide "pulse" messages to detect and ensure connectivity between the NameNode* and the data nodes.

When a pulse is not detected, *NameNode* strips the data node mapping from the *cluster* and continues to operate as if nothing had happened.

When the pulse returns, or a new pulse appears, the node is added to the cluster transparently to the user or application.

As with all file systems, data integrity is a key feature. HDFS supports a number of features designed to provide data integrity. As one might expect, when files are divided into blocks and then distributed across different servers in the *cluster*, any variation in the operation of any element could affect the integrity of the data. HDFS uses transaction logs and checksum validation to ensure integrity across the *cluster*.

Transaction logs are a very common practice in file system and database design. They keep track of each operation and are effective in auditing or rebuilding the system file if something unpleasant occurs.

Checksum validations are used to ensure the contents of files in HDFS. When a client requests a file, it verifies the contents by examining the checksum. If the checksum is correct, the file operation can continue. Otherwise, an error is reported. Checksum files are hidden to help prevent tampering.

DataNodes use local disks on the commodity server for persistence. All data blocks are stored locally, primarily for performance reasons.

5.3.2   Hadoop MapReduce.

MapReduce was designed by Google with the main objective of processing a large amount of data in batch, with superior efficiency, using a certain set of functions.

A component known as a "map" distributes the execution of parts or segments of programs and controls the sequencing of task execution in order to manage interdependent partial completions and failure recovery.

After distributed computing is complete, another function known as "reduce" comes into play that reaggregates all the elements to finally provide a result.

A very simple example of using MapReduce is counting words in a large number of different documents. Without using MapReduce, the developer would have to solve a number of problems that are inherent to parallel data processing.

To understand the capabilities of Hadoop MapReduce, we need to differentiate between MapReduce (the algorithm) and an implementation of MapReduce. The Hadoop MapReduce is an implementation of the algorithm developed and maintained by the Apache Hadoop project.

The best way to interpret this application is to view it as a MapReduce engine, because that's exactly how it works. From the data provided in an input, the engine converts fuel into output quickly and efficiently.

Hadoop MapReduce includes several stages, each with an important set of operations that are performed to achieve the primary goal of producing the Big Data answers, achieving the customer's goal.

The process begins with a request from the user to run a MapReduce program and continues until the results produced are sent to HDFS.

HDFS and MapReduce perform their work on nodes in a *cluster* hosted on commodity server racks. To simplify the issue, the diagram shows only two nodes.

When a client requests to run a MapReduce program, the first step is to locate and read the input file that contains the raw data. The file format is completely random, but the data must be converted to something that the program is capable of processing. These are the functions performed by *InputFormat* and *RecordReader* (RR).

The InputFormat function decides how the file will be broken into small chunks for processing using a function called *InputSplit*. It then assigns a *RecordReader* to transform the raw data for processing by the map.

The map has two inputs: a key and a value. Several types of *RecordReaders* are provided with Hadoop, offering a wide variety of conversion options. This feature is one of the ways that Hadoop uses to manage the wide variety of data types found in big data problems.

The data is now in an acceptable form to map. For each input pair, a distinct map instance is called to process the data. But what does it do with the processed output, and how can you know what it is doing? The map has two additional features to answer these questions.

Since *Map* and *Reduce* need to work together to process the data, the program needs to collect the output from the independent mappers and pass it on to the reducers. This task is performed by an *OutputCollector*.

The *Reporter* role also provides information collected from map tasks so that you know when or if map tasks are complete. This task is performed by an OutputCollector.

All of these jobs are being performed on multiple nodes in the Hadoop cluster simultaneously. There may be cases where outputs from a given mapping process need to be accumulated before scale-down can be initiated. Or cases where some of the intermediate results may need to be processed before reduction.

In addition, some of this output may be on a different node than the node where the reducers for that particular output will be executed. Gathering and shuffling intermediate results are performed by a partitioner and a classifier.

Mapping jobs will deliver the results to a specific partition as inputs for reduction jobs. After all map tasks are completed, the intermediate results are gathered in the partition and a shuffle occurs, sorting the output for optimal processing by reduction.

For each output pair the reduction is called to accomplish its task. In a similar way to mapping, shrinking gathers its output while all tasks are being processed.

Scale-in cannot begin until all mapping is done, and it is not complete until all instances are complete. The output of reduce is also a key and a value. While this is necessary for shrinking to do its job, it may not be the most effective output format for your application.

Hadoop provides the *OutputFormat feature that* works very similarly to *InputFormat*. The *OutputFormat* takes the key-value pair and arranges the output for writing to HDFS.

The last task is to actually write the data to HDFS. This is accomplished by *RecordWriter* and performs similarly to *RecordReader*. It takes the data to *the OutputFormat* and writes it to HDFS in the format required for the application program's requirements.

Coordination of all of these activities was managed in previous versions of Hadoop by a task scheduler. This programmer was rudimentary, and as the job mix changed and grew, it was found that a different approach was needed.

The main shortcoming of the old scheduler was the lack of resource management. The latest version of Hadoop has this new functionality.

Hadoop MapReduce is the heart of the Hadoop system. It provides all the features needed to break large data into manageable chunks, process the data in parallel in your distributed *cluster*, and then make the data available to the user.

And it does all this work in a highly fault-tolerant environment. The Hadoop ecosystem is a growing set of tools and technologies specifically designed to segment large data sets.

5.4 Hadoop and its ecosystem.

Hadoop MapReduce and Hadoop Distributed File System (HDFS) are powerful technologies designed to address the challenges of large data sets. That's the good news. The bad news is that your company really needs to have a team of programmers or data scientists to get the most out of these elemental components.

Commercial and open source developers around the world have been building and testing tools to increase Hadoop adoption and usability. Many are working on parts of the ecosystem and offering their improvements back to the Apache project. This constant stream of fixes and improvements helps to drive the entire ecosystem forward in a controlled and safe way.

Facing the challenge of processing large data sets without a super toolbox full of technologies and services is like trying to empty the ocean with a spoon. As core components, Hadoop MapReduce and HDFS are constantly being improved and provide great starting points, but something else is needed.

The Hadoop ecosystem provides an ever-growing collection of tools and technologies purpose-built to facilitate the development, deployment, and support of big data solutions. Before we focus on the key components of the ecosystem, let's break down the Hadoop ecosystem and the role it plays on the Big Data stage.

No building is stable without a foundation. While important, stability is not the only important criterion in a building. Each part of the building must collaborate for the final purpose. The walls, floors, stairs, electrical network, plumbing and roof need to complement each other, each trusts the other and all rely on the foundation for support and integration.

The same is true of the Hadoop ecosystem. They provide the basic framework and integration services needed to support key big data solution requirements. The rest of the ecosystem provides the components needed to build and manage real-world data-driven Big Data applications.

In the absence of the ecosystem, it would be up to developers, database administrators, system and network managers to structure their own ecosystem composed of a set of technologies to build and deploy Big Data solutions.

This is the case when companies want to adapt new technologies and emerging trends. The task of bringing technologies together in a new market is daunting. That's why the Hadoop ecosystem is so critical to Big Data success. It is the most comprehensive collection of tools and technologies available today to address Big Data challenges. The ecosystem facilitates the creation of new opportunities for the widespread adoption of Big Data by companies.

Task scheduling and tracking are integral parts of Hadoop MapReduce.

5.4.1   YARN = ResourceManager + ApplicationMaster.

YARN, as seen earlier, is one of the four core modules of Hadoop and provides the following services:

- Global Resource Management (*ResourceManager*)

- Per-Application Management (*ApplicationMaster*)

The intelligence of work and collaboration in YARN is as follows:

- The ResourceManager is a central management and control NodeManager on each of the nodes of a Hadoop cluster.

- It includes the Scheduler, whose only task is to allocate system resources to run specific applications. It is not responsible for monitoring or controlling the status of applications.

- All the information necessary for the system to perform its tasks is stored in the Resource Container, such as the CPU, disk, and network consumption information of the applications running on the node and in the cluster.

- Each node has a NodeManager slave from the ResourceManager set in the cluster.

- NodeManager monitors CPU, disk, network, and memory consumption and sends this information to the ResourceManager.

- For each application running on the node, there is a corresponding ApplicationMaster.

- If more resources are needed to sustain the running application, the ApplicationMaster notifies the NodeManager that it negotiates additional resources with the Scheduler in the ResourceManager for the application or negotiates with the Scheduler in the ResourceManager to release additional resources for the application.

- NodeManager is also responsible for monitoring the progress of running applications on the node.

5.4.2   HBase – columnar data making a difference.

HBase[23] is a distributed, non-relational database that uses HDFS as its persistence store. It was designed from Google BigTable and is capable of hosting very large tables, with billions of columns and rows. This

---

[23] HBase is an open-source, column-oriented distributed database, modeled after Google BigTable and written in Java.

capability is derived from its structure that is based on the layers of Hadoop clusters.

HBase provides random read and write access to data, in real time, for Big Data. It is highly configurable, providing great flexibility to handle large amounts of data. HBase is a columnar database where all data is stored in tables with rows and columns similar to RDBMSs.

The intersection of a row and a column is called a cell. The main difference between HBase tables and RDBMS tables is versioning. Each cell includes a *version*[24] attribute, which is a timestamp that uniquely identifies the cell. Versioning tracks changes in the cell and makes it possible to retrieve any version of the content if necessary.

HBase stores the data in cells in descending order (using the timestamp), so a read will always find the most recent values first.

Columns in HBase are organized into column families. The family name is used as a prefix to identify your family members. For example, color: white and color: blue are members of the color family.

HBase implementations are organized by column family, which makes it important to be fully aware of how data is being accessed and how large the columns can be.

Rows in HBase tables also have a key associated with them. The key structure is very flexible. The key can be a calculated value, text, or even another data structure. The key is used to control access to the cells in the row, and they are stored in ascending order of value.

All these features together constitute the scheme. The schema is defined and created before any data can be stored. Even so, tables can be changed and new column families can be added after the database is up and running. This extensibility is extremely useful when dealing

---

[24] From English version, versioning.

with big data because you can't always know in advance what the variety of your data streams is.

5.4.3   Hive - Big Data Mining.

Hive is a batch-driven data storage layer built on top of the core elements of Hadoop, HDFS, and MapReduce. It provides users who have mastered SQL with a simple SQL-lite implementation called HiveQL without sacrificing access through mappers and reducers.

With Hive, you can get the best of both worlds: access to structured data via SQL and sophisticated big data analysis with MapReduce.

Unlike most data warehouses, Hive is not designed for quick responses to queries. In fact, queries can take several minutes or even hours, depending on the complexity.

Hive is best used for mining data and deeper analysis that doesn't require real-time responses because it relies on the Hadoop foundation. But it has significant advantages, such as being extensible, scalable, and resilient, something that the average data warehouse is not.

Hive uses three mechanisms for data organization:

- Tables.

The tables here are the same as the RDBMS tables, mapped to directories in the Hadoop HDFS file system. In addition, it supports tables stored in other native file systems.

- Partitions.

A table in Hive can support one or more partitions. These partitions are mapped to subdirectories in the file system and represent the data distribution of the entire table. For example, if the table is called Hotels, with a key value of 12345 and a network value of Hilton, the path to the partition would be /hivewh/hotels/kv=12345/Hilton.

- Buckets.

The data is organized into buckets, which are stored as files in the directory partition on the file system. Buckets are hash-based *on* a column in the table.

Hive metadata is stored externally in a structure known as a *metastore*. Metastore is a relational database containing the detailed descriptions of Hive schemas, including columns, types, owners, key and value data, and statistical tables. The *metastore* is able to synchronize the data catalog with other metadata services in the Hadoop ecosystem.

5.4.4   Pig and Pig Latin.

The power and flexibility of Hadoop for big data is immediately visible to software developers because the Hadoop ecosystem was built by developers for developers.

However, not everyone is a software developer. *Pig* is designed to make Hadoop more accessible and usable by non-developers.

Pig is an interactive, script-based environment. Supporting the execution of *Pig* we have *Pig Latin*. A language used to express data flows. The *Pig Latin* language has the responsibility of performing the loading and processing of input data with a series of operators that transform the input data into the desired output.

The Pig runtime has two modes:

- Local mode where all scripts run on a single machine. Hadoop *MapReduce* and HDFS are not required.

- Hadoop. Also called *MapReduce* mode, all scripts run on a given Hadoop cluster.

Inside *Pig* creates a set of maps and reduction tasks. This way, the user doesn't have to worry about writing code, compiling packages, repackaging, presenting and retrieving the results. In many ways, *Pig* is analogous to SQL in the RDBMS world.

The *Pig Latin* language provides an abstract way to get answers from Big Data, focusing on the data rather than the structure of a custom software program.

Pig greatly simplifies prototyping tasks. As an example, we can cite the case where you need to run a *Pig* script on a small part of your Big Data environment to ensure that the results are what you want before committing to processing all the data.

Pig *programs* can run in three different ways, all of which support both local and Hadoop mode:

1. *Script*. A file containing Pig commands, identified by the suffix. pig. For example, file.pig or myscript.pig. The commands are interpreted by *Pig* and executed in sequential order.

2. Grunt. Grunt is a command interpreter. You can type *Pig Latin* into Grunt's command line and it will execute the command according to the expected result. This is very useful for prototyping and what-if scenarios.

3. Incorporated. *Pig* programs can be run as part of a Java program.

Pig *Latin* has a very rich syntax. Supports operators for the following operations:

*   Upload and store data.

*   Generate streaming data.

*   Filter data.

- Group and join data.

- Sort data.

- Combine and split data.

Pig Latin also supports a wide variety of types, expressions, functions, diagnostics, operators, macros, and file system commands. For more examples, visit the *Pig website* at Apache.com[25]. It is a rich resource that will provide you with all the details.

5.4.5 Sqoop.

Many companies store information in RDBMSs and databases, and they often need a way to move data from one to the other or from these databases to Hadoop.

While it is sometimes necessary to move data in real time, the most common is to upload or unload data in bulk. *Sqoop, SQL-to-Hadoop*, is a tool that provides the ability to extract data from non-Hadoop databases, transform it into a form usable by Hadoop, and then load it into HDFS.

This process is called ETL, for *Extract*, *Transform*, and *Load*. While receiving the data in Hadoop is critical for processing using MapReduce, it is also critical to obtain data from external Hadoop data sources for use in other types of applications. *Sqoop* is able to do this very well.

Like Pig, Sqoop is a command-line interpreter. You type Sqoop commands into the interpreter and they are executed one at a time. Sqoop has four main features:

---

[25] pig.apache.org.

- Bulk import. Sqoop can import individual tables or entire databases into HDFS. The data is stored in the native directories and files in the HDFS File System.

- Direct entry. Sqoop can import and map SQL (relational) databases directly into Hive and HBase.

- Data interaction. Sqoop can generate Java classes so that you can interact with the data programmatically.

- Data export. Sqoop can export data directly from HDFS to a relational database by defining the generated table based on the specifications of the target database.

Sqoop works by examining the database you want to import and selecting an appropriate import function for the source data. After acknowledging the input, it then reads the metadata from the table (or database) and creates a class definition of its input requirements.

You can force Sqoop to be selective so that you get only the columns you're looking for before input, rather than bringing in an entire table and then searching for its data. This can save you a lot of time.

The actual import from the external database to HDFS is performed by a MapReduce job created behind the scenes by Sqoop. Sqoop is another effective tool for non-programmers.

An important point to note is that one should rely on technologies such as HDFS and MapReduce. This is true of every element of the Hadoop ecosystem.

5.4.6   Zookeeper.

Hadoop's trump card for dealing with *Big Data challenges* is its divide and conquer philosophy. After the problem has been broken down, the achievement is based on the ability to employ parallel and distributed processing techniques in the *Hadoop* cluster.

For some *Big Data* problems, interactive tools are unable to provide reliable data or the opportunity needed to make business decisions. In these cases, you need to separate the applications into distributed tasks to solve these problems. Zookeeper is the Hadoop way to coordinate all elements of these distributed applications

Zookeeper as a technology is really simple, but its features are powerful. Arguably, it would be difficult, if not impossible, to build resilient and fault-tolerant distributed Hadoop applications without it.

Some of Zookeeper's capabilities are:

- Process synchronization. Zookeeper coordinates the start and stop of multiple nodes in the *cluster*. This ensures that all processing takes place in the order intended. When an entire process group is completed, then, and only then, can subsequent processing take place.

- Configuration management. *Zookeeper* can be used to send configuration attributes to any or all nodes in the *cluster*. When processing is dependent on particular resources that are available on all nodes, *Zookeeper* ensures consistency of configurations.

- Self-election. The *Zookeeper* understands the composition of the group and can assign a "leader" role to one of the nodes. This leader handles all client requests on behalf of the *cluster*. If the leader node fails, another leader will be elected from the remaining nodes.

- Reliable messaging. Even though the workloads in *Zookeeper* are loosely coupled, there is still a need for communication between nodes in the specific set for application distribution. *Zookeeper* offers a publish and subscribe feature that allows you to create a queue. This queue guarantees message deliveries even in the event of a node failure.

Because *Zookeeper* manages a variety of components, such as node groups and distributed applications, it is best implemented in racks. The reason is simple. The *Zookeeper* needs to be well-performing, resilient, and fault-tolerant at a level above the cluster itself. As a Hadoop cluster is already very fault tolerant, with the performance of *Zookeeper* it will recover on its own.

Zookeeper only has to worry about his own fault tolerance. The Hadoop ecosystem and supported commercial distributions are constantly changing. New tools and technologies are introduced, existing technologies are improved, and some technologies are replaced. This is one of the biggest advantages of open source.

Another is the adoption of open-source technologies by commercial companies. These companies enhance the products, making them better for everyone by offering support and services at a modest cost. That's how the Hadoop ecosystem has evolved and become a good choice to help solve *your company's* Big Data challenge.

5.5 Apache Hadoop at a glance.

1. Key Subproject Development

2. Apache SADH.[26] The primary storage system, which uses multiple replicas of data blocks, performs distribution across the nodes of a cluster and provides high access to application data.

3. Apache Hadoop MapReduce. A programming model and software framework for applications that performs distributed processing

---

[26] Hadoop Distributed File System.

of large data sets in compute clusters.

4. Apache Hadoop Common. Utilities that support the Hadoop framework, including File Systems (an abstract base class for a generic file system), remote procedure calls (CPR), and serialization libraries.

5. Apache Avro. Data serialization system.

6. Apache Cassandra. Scalable database with no single point of failure.

7. Apache Chukwa. Data collection system for monitoring systems. built on the basis of SADH and MapReduce. Includes a tool for displaying, monitoring, and analyzing results.

8. Apache HBase. Scalable, distributed database that supports structured data storage for large tables. Used for random access to read and write Big Data in real time.

9. Apache Hive. Storage system infrastructure that provides summary, ad hoc questions, and analysis of large data sets on file systems that support Hadoop files.

10. Apache Mahout. A scalable machine learning and data mining library with implementation of a wide range of algorithms, including clustering, sorting, collaborative filtering, and frequent mining pattern.

11. Apache Pig. A high-level data flow execution and language framework for parallel data analysis expression.

12. Apache *ZooKeeper*. A high-performance, centralized coordination service that maintains configuration and naming information and provides distributed synchronization and group services for distributed applications.

6 Big Data Analytics.

Big Data Analytics is one of the *buzzwords*[27] that has become one of the most popular buzzwords in the IT industry. It is a combination of "Big Data" and "Deep Analysis":

- Big Data, as already discussed, is the phenomenon of the increase in data traffic made possible by Web2.0, in which a lot of data from user transactions and activities is collected and can be mined to extract useful information.

- Analytics is an approach derived from the use of advanced mathematical and statistical techniques to build models from data.

An interesting feature of Big Data Analytics is that these two areas are quite different and disconnected, and the people who work in each area have a very different background.

With the increasing evolution of digital transformation, Big Data Analytics has become one of the most promising technologies for the business world. Its importance is associated with a series of benefits, both for improving strategies and processes, as well as for increasing sales and revenue.

Big Data Analytics processing has the following profile:

- Usually carried out in batches.

- Usually at night.

  - Once a day.

---

[27] Buzzword. It is the postmodern term that defines the words that are "fashionable" within a certain universe, whether or not they define new things. "Buzzword" is also a buzzword.

- Usually, at different stages of this batch process.

The elements on the left correspond to Big Data. These are applications typically run using the Hadoop/PIG/Hive technology platform with implementation of classic ETL logic.

By leveraging the MapReduce model that Hadoop provides, we can linearly scale processing by adding more machines to the Hadoop cluster. Designing cloud computing resources (e.g., Amazon EMR) is a very common approach to accomplish these types of tasks.

The deep analysis part, the group of elements on the right, is usually done in R, SPSS, SAS using a much smaller amount of carefully sampled data that fits the capacity of a single machine. They typically total less than a few hundred thousand data records.

The deep analysis part usually involves data visualization, data preparation, model learning, linear regression and regularization, K-nearest neighbor/support vector machine/Bayesian network/neural network, decision tree and set methods, and model evaluation.

It is no coincidence that some companies have already taken the lead and invested US$ 187 billion in Big Data Analytics in 2019, according to IDC[28].

And it is already a certainty in the market that companies like Amazon and Google have consolidated themselves as masters in Big Data analysis. They use the resulting knowledge to gain a competitive advantage. Take the case of Amazon's product recommendation processing.

The company gathers the customer's purchase history, their searches and the information they have about them to bring suggestions that

---

[28] International Data Corporation. https://www.idc.com/

always have a great relationship with their needs. It is an excellent marketing machine, based on Big Data Analytics, which has proven to be extremely successful.

The ability to analyze large volumes of data offers unique opportunities for the company, as it is possible to move from an analysis limited to examples or data samples to large sets that translate the behavior of the entire universe (Lavalle, 2010).

Evolving in concepts, we have that Big Data analysis is:

• A technology-based strategy that enables the collection of deeper, more relevant insights from customers, partners, and the business—thereby gaining a competitive advantage.

• Working with datasets whose size and variety are beyond the capturing, storing, and analysis capabilities of typical database software (Helbing, 2015a).

• Processing a continuous stream of data in real time, enabling time-sensitive decision-making faster than at any other time (Pavlo et al., 2009).

• Distributed in nature. Analytics processing goes where the data is for greater speed and efficiency.

• A new paradigm in which IT collaborates with business users and "data scientists" to identify and implement analytics that increase operational efficiency and solve new business problems (Yoon, 2011).

• Shift decision-making within the company and enable people to make better, faster, real-time decisions.

And that Big Data analytics is not:

• Technology only. At the enterprise level, it refers to exploiting vastly improved data sources to gain insights.

• Volume only. It also refers to variety and speed. But, perhaps more importantly, it refers to the value derived from data.

• A technology used only by large online companies such as Google or Amazon. While internet companies may have pioneered Big Data on the web scale, applications reach every industry.

• Use of traditional "one-size-fits-all" relational databases built on shared disk and memory architecture. Big Data Analytics uses a network of computing resources for massively parallel processing (PMP).

• A replacement for relational databases or data centers. Structured data remains of critical importance to businesses. However, traditional systems may not be able to handle the new sources and contexts of Big Data (Mcafee et., 2012).

Unfortunately, as we know, analyzing large volumes of data is a major challenge.

When dealing with large volumes of data, the first question to ask, before diving into this problem, is:

–   What problem does the company need to solve?

The company may not be sure about what is possible to do with a lot of data, but it already knows that data has a lot of potential, and certainly patterns can emerge from this data before it is understood why it is there.

This type of thinking will lead the team to have a sense of what is possible with the data. An example that applies to all e-commerce businesses is the interest in predicting customer behavior to avoid churn.

6.1   Types of Big Data Analytics.

The high-level type of problem will drive the Big Data analysis process. Alternatively, in case one is unsure of the business problems, it may be necessary to examine the areas of the company that need improvement (Stonebraker, 2012).

Types:

1. Descriptive analysis.

   Tools in this class tell companies what happened. They create simple reports and visualizations that show what happened at a particular point in time or over a period of time. These are the least advanced analytical tools.

2. Diagnostic analysis.

   Diagnostic tools that explain why something happened. More advanced than descriptive reporting tools, they allow analysts to dive deep into the data and determine the root causes for a given situation.

3. Predictive analytics.

   Among the most popular Big Data analytics tools available today, predictive analytics tools use highly advanced algorithms to predict what might happen next. Often, these tools use artificial intelligence and machine learning technology.

4. Prescriptive analysis.

   A step above predictive analytics, prescriptive analytics tells companies what they must do to achieve their desired outcome. These tools require very advanced machine learning capabilities, and few solutions on the market today offer true prescriptive capabilities.

6.2   What is *data mining*[29] ?

The direct translation of data mining already helps us understand what it is about. It is a process that aims to examine large volumes of data in order to find consistent patterns. When they are found, these patterns must go through a validation process to become usable information.

It is a fact that, due to the enormous amount of data to be validated, data mining cannot be carried out effectively with human action alone (Kandalkar, 2014). Therefore, this is one of the points that make digital transformation essential for the development of companies.

With the automatic use of learning algorithms, data mining is able to demonstrate interactions and consumption trends presented by a company's consumers, all in a reasonable time (Armstrong, 2006).

Thus, this concept is nothing more than a collection of techniques that allow filtering from Big Data the data considered important to achieve a certain objective.

The techniques used originate from the study of statistics and artificial intelligence, with a little database management. Generally, the objective of data mining is to classify data or predict some situation based on the processed data (Van Aalst et. Al, 2010).

In classification, the idea is to classify the data into groups. For example, a merchant might be interested in the characteristics of customers who consumed a product because of a promotion and customers who visited the promotion but didn't consume the product. These clients comprise two classes (Vaishnavi et al., 2004).

In forecasting, the idea is to predict the future behavior of a variable. In the same example, the merchant may be interested in predicting

---

[29] Data mining. A process that aims to examine large **volumes of data** in order to find consistent patterns.

which or how many customers will consume the product of a particular promotion.

Typical algorithms used in data mining include classification trees, logistic regression, neural networks, and clustering techniques with K-nearest neighbors.

6.2.1   Classification trees.

The rank tree is a very popular data mining technique. It is used to classify a dependent categorical variable based on the measurements of one or more predictor variables. The result is a tree with nodes and links between nodes that can be read to form if-then rules.

Take as an example of a rating tree the case of a cable company that wants to determine which customers are likely to cancel service.

The company has information such as:

- How long the customer has had the subscription.

- If he has had problems with the service.

- What is the package of the customer plan.

- What region of the country does he live in.

- How old is the customer.

- Whether there are additional products linked to the customer's package.

- Competitor information.

The software is expected to generate two groups of customers: permanent and potential loss.

The data is organized into two groups:

- Training data.

- Test data.

The algorithm runs by forming a tree based on a series of rules. For example, if customers have been with the company for more than ten years and they are over 55 years old, they are likely to remain loyal customers.

Advanced analytics don't require big data. However, being able to apply advanced analytics with Big Data can provide some important results.

6.2.2 Logistic regression.

It is a statistical technique that aims to produce, from a set of observations, a model that allows the prediction of values taken by a categorical variable, often binary, from a series of continuous and/or binary explanatory variables.

Logistic regression is widely used in the medical and social sciences, and has other names, such as the logistic model, the Logit model[30], and the maximum entropy classifier.

Logistic regression is used in areas such as the following:

- In medicine, it allows, for example, to determine the factors that characterize a group of sick individuals in relation to healthy individuals;

- In the field of insurance, it makes it possible to find fractions of the clientele which are sensitive to a particular insurance policy in relation to a particular risk;

---

[30] The logit model provides a statistical model that results in the probability that a dependent response variable is either 0 or 1.

- In financial institutions, it can detect the risk groups for the underwriting of a credit;

- In econometrics, it allows us to explain a discrete variable, such as voting intentions in electoral elections.

The success of logistic regression is justified above all by the numerous tools that allow for an in-depth interpretation of the results obtained.

6.2.3   Neural networks

Neural networks are computing systems with interconnected nodes that function like the neurons of the human brain. Using algorithms, they can recognize hidden patterns and correlations in raw data, group and classify them, and – over time – continuously learn and improve.

Artificial neural networks are often presented as systems of "interconnected neurons, which can compute input values", simulating the behavior of biological neural networks.

The first neural network was conceived by Warren McCulloch and Walter Pitts in 1943. They wrote a seminal paper on how neurons should work, and then modeled their ideas by creating a simple neural network with electrical circuits.(McCulloch & Pitts, 1943)

This innovative model paved the way for neural network research in two areas.

AI research accelerated rapidly, but it wasn't until 1975 that Kunihiko Fukushima proposed the first true multilayer neural network.

The original goal of the neural network approach was to create a computational system capable of solving problems like a human brain. However, as time went on, researchers shifted their focus to using neural networks to solve specific tasks, deviating from a strictly biological approach.

Since then, neural networks have supported a wide range of tasks, including computer vision, speech recognition, machine translation, social media filtering, board or video games, and medical diagnostics.

As the volume of structured and unstructured data has increased to Big Data levels, people have developed *deep learning* systems that are essentially neural networks with many layers.

Deep learning enables the capture and mining of more and larger volumes of data, including unstructured data.

6.2.4 Clustering techniques with K-nearest neighbors.

It is a nonparametric classification method first developed by Evelyn Fix and Joseph Hodges in 1951, and later expanded by Thomas Cover.

It is used for classification and regression. In either case, the input consists of the closest k training examples in the dataset.

The output depends on whether k -NN is used for classification or regression:

- In the k-NN classification, the output is a class association. An object is ranked by a plurality of votes from its neighbors, with the object being assigned to the most common class among its k nearest neighbors (k is a positive, typically small integer). If k = 1, then the object is simply assigned to the class of that single nearest neighbor.

- In k-NN regression, the output is the value of the object's property. This value is the average of the values of the nearest neighbors. k -NN is a type of classification where the function is approximated only locally and all calculations are deferred until the function is evaluated.

Because this algorithm relies on distance for classification, if the features represent different physical units or come at very different scales, normalizing the training data can dramatically improve their accuracy.

7 Big Data *Analytics Governance.*

Big data governance is consolidating as an important part of the *analytics equation*.

Among the issues of business analysis, improvements will need to be made in governance solutions to ensure the veracity of new data sources, especially due to the merging with existing reliable data in the Data Warehouse.

Data security and privacy solutions also need to be enhanced to support management and control stored in new technologies.

When it comes to Big Data Analytics, it is necessary to be aware that when the work expands beyond the desktop, the algorithms used frequently will need to be redone, changing the internal code without affecting its external function.

The beauty of a Big Data infrastructure is that you can run a model that used to take hours or days in just a few minutes.

The approach of running analytics close to the data source reduces the amount of data to be stored by filtering out only the data that has value. It also allows you to analyze data earlier, looking for important events. This is critical for real-time decision-making.

In addition, vendors are starting to offer a new range of analytics designed to be placed close to data sources, allowing data to be analyzed without the need to store it first and then perform the analysis.

This approach of performing analysis closer to data sources also allows you to analyze data earlier, looking at key events, which is critical for real-time decision-making.

Of course, analytics will continue to evolve, as the good thing about this story is that this is an area of active research.

When it comes to Big Data, it is important that the platform meets the following requirements:

➢ Integrate technologies. The infrastructure needs to integrate new Big Data technologies with traditional technologies so that the suite is able to process all types of data and volumes and make them useful for traditional analytics.

➢ Store large amounts of disparate data. A Hadoop system may be required to process, store, and manage large amounts of data at rest, regardless of whether it is structured, semi-structured, or unstructured.

➢ Process data on the go. A stream computing capability may be required to process moving data that is continuously generated by sensors, smart devices, video, audio, and records to support real-time decision-making.

➢ Load data from Data Warehouse. You may need an optimized solution to process operational analytical workloads and manage the growing amounts of trusted data.

And, of course, it is necessary to have the ability to integrate the data you have with the results of Big Data analysis.

7.1   Examples of Big Data analytics that worked.

The effectiveness of Big Data has already been verified by many companies. In fact, it is because of the various success stories that this is a very interesting tool for companies that intend to increase the profitability of their business.

Some examples of success are:

• UPS. The logistics company UPS cross-referenced data from vehicle sensors, maps, geolocation and customer order requirements in order to reduce the distances traveled per year and, in this way, optimize the work of drivers. The use of Big Data generated savings of 85 million miles per year and a significant amount spent on fuel, in addition to increasing the quality of life of employees.

- Nike. Nike monitors the sports habits and behaviors of its audience through wearable applications and devices, known as *wearables*[31], which are capable of generating information related to distance traveled, speeds, preferred places for training, etc. With this, the company continues to create products that are increasingly aligned with the expectations of its target audience, building customer loyalty and winning over more and more athletes.

- Maplink. Maplink is a company specialized in the digitization of maps that, by testing a satellite tracking software that crossed the data generated by more than 400 thousand cars in São Paulo, was able to perform an accurate diagnosis of traffic indicating all the points of slowness, the reasons and the possible alternatives for drivers.

- Danone. When launching Greek yogurt on the market, Danone faced a huge problem with the product's shelf life, which is quite short. The use of Big Data was important to better understand the behavior of its consumers and start delivering to retail chains with better synchrony, reducing spending on expired products.

---

[31] Any and all technological devices that can be used as an accessory or that we can wear are wearable.

7.2   Text analysis and Big Data.

As discussed here in this book, most data is unstructured and includes information both internal and external to the company, such as documents, emails, tweets, blogs, YouTube videos, and satellite imagery.

The amount and variety of this data is growing rapidly day by day. Increasingly, companies want to take advantage of this wealth of data to understand the implications of consumer change for their business today and in the future. While image and audio analysis are still in their early stages, text analysis is evolving to become a mainstream technology.

An example of how a company was able to use text analysis to leverage decision-making is the case of a large car manufacturer that needed to improve the quality of its cars that were presenting many problems. She found that by analyzing repairs made at authorized service partners' workshops, she could identify quality problems in their cars as they enter the market.

The company adopted this analysis as an early warning system. The sooner it is able to identify problems, the sooner it can change the production line to have more satisfied customers

Before using text analytics, the company explored information from its network of authorized repair shops, including part numbers and defect codes. This worked well enough for many years, but only for the problems that the company already knew existed.

However, the system was not useful for revealing problems hidden throughout the service process that were only known to the people who interacted with customers. The texts of the Facebook, Instagram and Twitter posts were used to identify the posts related to the cars and services in question.

Undoubtedly, the data collected and analyzed was much greater than expected, and most of it was disregarded.

In this case, text analytics has been adopted and continues to be used in a wide variety of Big Data use cases, from social media analytics to warranty analytics and fraud analytics.

What differentiates unstructured data from structured data is that its structure is unpredictable.

As mentioned earlier, some people believe that the phrase unstructured data is misleading because each text may contain its own specific structure or formatting based on the software that created it. In fact, it's the content of the document that's really unstructured.

Think about the types of text that exist and the structure that can be associated with each one:

1. Documents:

    "SEVENTH CLAUSE: The works and expenses with the conservation, cleaning and cleanliness of the property will be at the expense, risk and expense of the LESSEE, who is obliged to return the property in perfect conditions of cleanliness, cleanliness, conservation and painting, when this agreement ends or is terminated, without any pecuniary liability for the LESSOR. The LESSEE may not carry out major works or modify the structure of the property leased herein, without prior written authorization from the RENTAL FIRM. If the LESSEE consents to the execution of the works, they will be immediately incorporated into the property, without the LESSEE being entitled to any compensation for the works or retention for improvements. Removable improvements may be removed, as long as they do not disfigure the leased property."

2. Emails:

"Good afternoon Dr. João,

I hereby apply for the vacancy of programmer, according to the advertisement published on the Emprego.com website.

Attached is my curriculum vitae, as well as my cover letter, explaining the reasons for my application.

Any question, please feel free to contact me. I am available for any clarification.

Best regards, ..."

3. Log Files:

222.222.222.222-- [08/Oct/2012:11:11:54-0400] "GET/HTTP/1.1" 200 10801
"http://www.google.com/search?q=log+analyzer&ie=.... . .

4. Tweets:

#O book by Prof. Marcão explains everything about Big Data!

Clearly, some of these examples have more structure than others. For example, a clause in a lease agreement has some structure in terms of sentences and the model it can follow. An email can have little structure. A log file can have its own structure. A tweet can have abbreviations or strange characters.

The big question is then:

- How can you analyze data that has structures that are so different from each other or that have no structure at all?

There are numerous methods for analyzing unstructured data. Historically, these techniques came outside of technical areas such as natural language processing[32], knowledge discovery, data mining, information retrieval, and statistics.

Text analysis is the process of analyzing unstructured text to extract relevant information, transforming it into structured information that can then be leveraged in a variety of ways.

The processes of analysis and extraction take advantage of techniques that originated in computational linguistics, statistics, and other information science disciplines.

The text analysis process uses various algorithms, such as sentence structure understanding, to analyze the unstructured text and then extract information and transform that information into data structures.

Note that we're focusing on text extraction, not keyword research. Search consists of retrieving a document based on what end users already know they are looking for. Text analysis is all about discovering information.

Although text analysis is different from search, it can augment search techniques. For example, text analysis combined with search can be used to provide better categorization or classification of documents and to produce summaries.

There is no doubt that for most commercial companies, optimizing the customer experience and maximizing customer retention are powerful guidelines for many companies.

---

[32] Natural Language Processing NLP. Natural Language Processing (NLP) is a branch of artificial intelligence that helps computers understand, interpret, and manipulate human language. NLP results from diverse disciplines, including computer science and computational linguistics, that seek to bridge the gap between human communication and the understanding of computers.

Companies that care about their future are constantly concerned with core issues, such as:

- What do customers want and aren't finding on our website?

- What are the main areas of customer complaints?

- What are the complaints about our partners?

- What is the level of customer satisfaction with specific services?

- What are the most frequent issues that lead to customer churn?

- What are the main segments that offer the greatest sales potential?

The sources of information that can contribute to building answers to these questions are on the internet, such as:

- Emails sent by customers to the company.

- In satisfaction surveys.

- Grades assigned to the *call center*.

- Internal documents.

- Comments on Facebook.

- Instagram posts.

- Comments on Twitter.

Text analytics can help identify and address the causes of customer dissatisfaction in a timely manner and can help improve the company's image by resolving issues before they become a major customer beheading.

But there is a question here. Is this really a Big Data problem? The answer is it depends. It mainly depends on the volume of data involved in the problem and how real-time the company wants to analyze the problems. If there is a large volume of data that is delivered in batch, the company may want to merge this data with structured data, as we have discussed earlier.

7.3   Characteristics of Big Data Analytics.

It is important to be clear that Big Data analysis must be seen from two perspectives:

1. Decision-oriented.

   Similar to traditional business intelligence, it focuses on selective subsets and representations of larger data sources in order to apply the results in decision-making.

   Certainly these decisions can result in some kind of action or process of change, but the purpose of the analysis is to support the decision made.

2. Action-oriented.

   Used for a quick response, when a pattern emerges or specific types of data are detected and action is required.

   Users have the possibility to take advantage of this exceptional feature of Big Data, through analysis with current data, and cause changes in their business decisions.

Finding and utilizing Big Data by building analytics applications may hold the key to extracting value sooner rather than later. One problem with the creation of applications is whether it is more effective to build these custom applications from scratch or to take advantage of platforms and/or components available on the market.

To contribute to this analysis, we will initially examine some additional characteristics of Big Data analytics that make it different from traditional types of analysis, in addition to the three Vs of volume, velocity, and variety. These characteristics are organized in the following figure.

In many cases, Big Data Analytics will be presented to the end user as a set of reports and visualizations, because the raw data may be incomprehensible to them.

It will be necessary to have tools and presentation techniques to make the data meaningful. DW-generated reports are already familiar to users, but with new tools, data that was previously presented in static reports can provide new insights or create new opportunities for analysis.

Data visualization techniques can be useful, but they will also have to be improved or supported by more sophisticated tools to make large volumes of data understandable.

Early adoption of big data requires building new applications designed to meet analytics requirements and deadlines.

Characteristic	Detailing
Programmable	With a large volume of data to analyze, it is possible to start with raw data that can be processed programmatically or do some kind of exploration due to the size of the data mass.
Data-driven	Instead of using hypotheses to analyze the data, you can use the data itself to conduct the analysis.
Variety of attributes	In the past, you had hundreds of attributes or characteristics in the source data. Now you may have to work with hundreds of gigabytes

		of data consisting of thousands of attributes and millions of observations.
	Iterative	By means of computation, it is possible to iterate on the models until the desired path is obtained.
	Rapidity	With infrastructure-as-a-service (IaaS) platforms, such as Amazon Cloud Services (ACS), you can quickly create a *cluster* of machines to process large data sets and analyze them quickly.

These new applications can be classified into two classes:

1. Custom.

   Coded from scratch. They are created for a specific purpose or for a related set of purposes.

   Certain areas of a company will always require a customized set of technologies to support unique activities or provide a competitive advantage.

2. Semi-personalized.

   Based on existing structures or components.

   Even if new toolsets continue to be available to help the business manage and analyze big data more effectively, it may not be possible to get what you want with what is already available.

8   Conclusion.

Throughout this book, Simplifying Big Data in 7 Chapters, we explore the essential fundamentals of Big Data, demystifying concepts and presenting practical tools to turn data into strategic value.

We started with the definition and pillars of Big Data, went through the fundamental steps for the success of projects in the area, and unraveled the impact of tools such as Hadoop and Big Data Analytics.

We also address the myths and trends shaping the future of technology and highlight the importance of data governance to ensure quality and ethics in the use of information.

This knowledge is just the beginning. This book provides a solid foundation for understanding Big Data, but the journey to mastering this area goes much further. For those who want to deepen their knowledge, understand new tools, and explore specific applications, the Big Data collection is an indispensable resource.

This book is just an initial step in a transformative journey.

This volume is part of a larger collection, Big Data, that connects the universe of Big Data to the fascinating world of artificial intelligence. The other books in the collection explore crucial topics such as machine learning, predictive analytics, intelligent systems integration, and the use of advanced algorithms for decision-making.

Each volume is designed to provide in-depth, actionable insight, allowing you to broaden your horizons and understand how Big Data and AI can transform your operations and strategies.

By purchasing and exploring the other books in the collection, available on Amazon, you will have access to a comprehensive guide that combines theory and practice, technology and strategy, empowering you to stand out in an increasingly data- and artificial intelligence-driven market.

The Big Data journey has only just begun. Keep exploring and turn the power of data to your greatest advantage.

9 Bibliography.

ACQUISTI, A., BRANDIMARTE, L., & LOEWENSTEIN, G. (2015). Privacy and human behavior in the age of information. Science, 347(6221), 509-514. Available at: https://www.heinz.cmu.edu/~acquisti/papers/Acquisti-Science-Privacy-Review.pdf.

ACQUISTI, A., TAYLOR, C., & WAGMAN, L. (2016). The economics of privacy. Journal of Economic Literature, 54(2), 442-92.

AKIDAU, Tyler, CHERNYAK, Slava, LAX, Reuven. (2019). Streaming Systems: The What, Where, When, and How of Large-Scale Data Processing.

ALGORITHMWATCH. (2019) Automating Society 2019. Available at: https://algorithmwatch.org/en/automating-society-2019/

ARMSTRONG, M. (2006). Competition in two-sided markets. The RAND Journal of Economics.

ARMSTRONG, M. (2006). Competition in two-sided markets. The RAND Journal of Economics, 37(3), 668-691.

BELKIN, N.J. (1978). Information concepts for information science. Journal of Documentation, v. 34, n. 1, p. 55-85.

BOLLIER, D., & Firestone, C. M. (2010). The promise and peril of Big Data. Washington, DC: Aspen Institute, Communications and Society Program.

BOYD, D; CRAWFORD, K. (2012). Critical Questions for Big Data: Provocations for a Cultural, Technological, and Scholarly Phenomenon. Information, Communication, & Society v.15, n.5, p. 662-679.

BRETON, P. & PROULX S. (1989). L'explosion de la communication. la naissance d'une nouvelle idéologie. Paris: La Découverte.

BUBENKO, J. A., WANGLER, B. (1993). "Objectives Driven Capture of Business Rules and of Information System Requirements". IEEE Systems Man and Cybernetics'93 Conference, Le Touquet, France.

CHEN, H., CHIANG, R. H., & STOREY, V. C. (2012). Business Intelligence and Analytics: From Big Data to Big Impact. MIS Quarterly.

CHENG, Y., Qin, C., & RUSU, F. (2012). Big Data Analytics made easy. SIGMOD '12 Proceedings of the 2012 ACM SIGMOD International Conference on Management of Data New York.

COHEN, Reuven. (2012). Brazil's Booming Business of Big Data – Available at: https://www.forbes.com/sites/reuvencohen/2012/12/12/brazil s-booming-business-of-bigdata/?sh=1de7e6bc4682

COMPUTERWORLD. (2016) Ten cases of Big Data that guaranteed a significant return on investment. Available at: https://computerworld.com.br/plataformas/10-casos-de-big-data-que-garantiram-expressivo-retorno-sobre-investimento/.

DAVENPORT, T. H. (2014). Big Data at work: debunking myths and uncovering opportunities. Rio de Janeiro: Elsevier.

DAVENPORT, T; PATIL, D. (2012). Data scientist: the sexiest job of the 21st century. Harvard Business Review. Available at: https://hbr.org/2012/10/data-scientist-the-sexiest-job-of-the-21st-century.

DAVENPORT, T; PATIL, D. (2012). Data scientist: the sexiest job of the 21st century. Harvard Business Review. Available at: https://hbr.org/2012/10/data-scientist-the-sexiest-job-of-the-21st-century.

DIXON, James. 2010. Pentaho, Hadoop, and Data Lakes. Blog, October. Available at:

https://jamesdixon.wordpress.com/2010/10/14/pentaho-hadoop-and-data-lakes/

EDWARD Choi, M. T. (2017). RETAIN: An Interpretable Predictive Model for Healthcare using Reverse Time Attention Mechanism. Available in https://arxiv.org/pdf/1608.05745.pdf

GLASS, R. ; CALLAHAN, (2015).S. The Big Data-Driven Business: How to Use Big Data to Win Customers, Beat Competitors, and Boost Profit. New Jersey: John Wiley & Sons, Inc.

GÓMEZ-BARROSO, J. L. (2018). Experiments on personal information disclosure: Past and future avenues. Telematics and Informatics, 35(5),   1473-1490.Available   at: https://doi.org/10.1016/j.tele.2018.03.017

GUALTIERI, M. (2013). Big Data Predictive Analytics Solutions. Massachusetts: Forrester.

HALPER, F. (2013). How To Gain Insight From Text. TDWI Checklist Report.

HALPER, F., & KRISHNAN, K. (2013). TDWI Big Data Maturity Model Guide Interpreting Your Assessment Score. TDWI Benchmark Guide 2013–2014.

HELBING, D. (2014). The World after Big Data: What the Digital Revolution   Means   for   Us.   Available   at: http://papers.ssrn.com/sol3/papers.cfm?abstract_id=2438957.

HELBING, D. (2015a). Big Data Society: Age of Reputation or Age of Discrimination?. In: HELBING, D. Thinking Ahead-Essays on Big Data, Digital Revolution, and Participatory Market Society. Springer International Publishing. p. 103-114.

HELBING, D. (2015b). Thinking Ahead-Essays on Big Data, Digital Revolution, and Participatory Market Society. Springer International Publishing.

HILBERT, M. (2013). Big Data for Development: From Information to Knowledge Societies. Available at https://www.researchgate.net/publication/254950835_Big_Dat a_for_Development_From_Information-_to_Knowledge_Societies.

IBM. (2014). Exploiting Big Data in telecommunications to increase revenue, reduce customer churn and operating costs. Source: IBM: http://www-01.ibm.com/software/data/bigdata/industry-telco.html.

INMON, W. H. (1992). Building the Data Warehouse. John Wiley & Sons, New York, NY, USA.

INMON, W. H. (1996). Building the Data Warehouse. John Wiley & Sons, New Yorkm NY, USA.2nd edition.

JARVELIN, K. & Vakkari, P. (1993) The evolution of Library and Information Science 1965-1985: a content analysis of journal articles. Information Processing & Management, v.29, n.1, p. 129-144.

KAMIOKA, T; TAPANAINEN, T. (2014). Organizational use of Big Data and competitive advantage - Exploration of Antecedents. Available at: https://www.researchgate.net/publication/284551664_Organiz ational_Use_of_Big_Data_and_Competitive_Advantage_-_Exploration_of_Antecedents.

KANDALKAR, N.A; WADHE, A. (2014). Extracting Large Data using Big Data Mining, International Journal of Engineering Trends and Technology. v. 9, n.11, p.576-582.

KIMBALL, R.; ROSS, M. (2013). The Data Warehouse Toolkit: The Definitive Guide to Dimensional Modeling, Third Edition. Wiley 10475 Crosspoint Boulevard Indianapolis, IN 46256: John Wiley & Sons, Inc.

KSHETRI, N. (2014). Big Data' s impact on privacy, security and consumer welfare. Telecommunications Policy, 38(11), 1134-1145.

LAVALLE, S., LESSER, E., SHOCKLEY, R., HOPKINS, M. S., & KRUSCHWITZ, N. (2010). Big Data, Analytics and the Path From Insights to Value.

LOHR, S. (2012). The Age of Big Data. The New York Times.

MACHADO, Felipe Nery Rodrigues. 2018. Database-Design and Implementation. [S.I.]: Editora Saraiva.

MANYIKA, J., CHUI, M., BROWN, B., BUGHIN, J., DOBBS, R., ROXBURGH, C., & BYERS, A. H. (2011). Big Data: The next frontier for innovation, competition, and productivity.

OHLHORST, J. F. (2012). Big Data Analytics: Turning Big Data into Big Money. Wiley.

OSWALDO, T., PJOTR, P., MARC, S., & RITSERT, C. J. (2011). Big Data, but are we ready? Available at: https://www.nature.com/articles/nrg2857-c1.

PAVLO, A., PAULSON, E., RASIN, A., ABADI, D. J., DEWITT, D. J., MADDEN, S., & STONEBRAKER, M. (2009). A comparison of approaches to large-scale data analysis. SIGMOD, pp. 165–178.

RAJ, P., & DEKA, G. C. (2012). Handbook of Research on Cloud Infrastructures for Big Data Analytics. Information Science: IGI Global.

SUBRAMANIAM, Anushree. 2020. What is Big Data? – A Beginner's Guide to the World of Big Data. Available at: edureka.co/blog/what-is-big-data/.

TANKARD, C. (2012). Big Data security, Network Security, Volume 2012, Issue7, July 2012, Pages 5 -8, ISSN 1353-4858.

TM FORUM. (2005). SLA management handbook - volume 2. Technical Report GB9712, TeleManagement Forum.

VAISHNAVI, V. K., & KUECHLER, W. (2004). Design Science Research in Information Systems.

VAN AALST, W. M., VAN HEE, K. M., VAN WERF, J. M., & VERDONK, M. (March 2010). Auditing 2.0: Using Process Mining to Support Tomorrow's Auditor. Computer (Volume:43, Issue:3.

WANG, Y., KUNG, L., & BYRD, T. A. (2018). Big Data analytics: Understanding its capabilities and potential benefits for healthcare organizations. Technological Forecasting and Social Change, 126, 3-13.

WIDJAYA, Ivan. (2019). What are the costs of big data? Available at: http://www.smbceo.com/2019/09/04/what-are-the-costs-of-big-data/

10 Big Data Collection: Unlocking the Future of Data in an Essential Collection.

The Big Data collection was created to be an indispensable guide for professionals, students, and enthusiasts who want to confidently navigate the vast and fascinating universe of data. In an increasingly digital and interconnected world, Big Data is not just a tool, but a fundamental strategy for the transformation of businesses, processes, and decisions. This collection sets out to simplify complex concepts and empower your readers to turn data into valuable insights.

Each volume in the collection addresses an essential component of this area, combining theory and practice to offer a broad and integrated understanding. You'll find themes such as:

In addition to exploring the fundamentals, the collection also looks into the future, with discussions on emerging trends such as the integration of artificial intelligence, text analytics, and governance in increasingly dynamic and global environments.

Whether you're a manager looking for ways to optimize processes, a data scientist exploring new techniques, or a beginner curious to understand the impact of data on everyday life, the Big Data collection is the ideal partner on this journey. Each book has been developed with accessible yet technically sound language, allowing readers of all levels to advance their understanding and skills.

Get ready to master the power of data and stand out in an ever-evolving market. The Big Data collection is available on Amazon and is the key to unlocking the future of data-driven intelligence.

10.1   Who is the Big Data collection for.

The Big Data collection is designed to cater to a diverse audience that shares the goal of understanding and applying the power of data in an increasingly information-driven world. Whether you're a seasoned professional or just starting your journey in the technology and data space, this collection offers valuable insights, practical examples, and indispensable tools.

1. Technology and Data Professionals.

Data scientists, data engineers, analysts, and developers will find in the collection the fundamentals they need to master concepts such as Big Data Analytics, distributed computing, Hadoop, and advanced tools. Each volume covers technical topics in a practical way, with clear explanations and examples that can be applied in everyday life.

2. Managers and Organizational Leaders.

For leaders and managers, the collection offers a strategic view on how to implement and manage Big Data projects. The books show how to use data to optimize processes, identify opportunities, and make informed decisions. Real-world examples illustrate how companies have used Big Data to transform their businesses in industries such as retail, healthcare, and the environment.

3. Entrepreneurs and Small Businesses.

Entrepreneurs and small business owners who want to leverage the power of data to improve their competitiveness can also benefit. The collection presents practical strategies for using Big Data in a scalable way, demystifying the idea that this technology is exclusive to large corporations.

4. Students and Beginners in the Area.

If you're a student or just starting to explore the universe of Big Data, this collection is the perfect starting point. With accessible language and practical examples, the books make complex concepts more understandable, preparing you to dive deeper into data science and artificial intelligence.

5. Curious and Technology Enthusiasts.

For those who, even outside of the corporate or academic environment, have an interest in understanding how Big Data is shaping the world, the collection offers a fascinating and educational introduction. Discover how data is transforming areas as diverse as health, sustainability, and human behavior.

Regardless of your level of expertise or the industry you're in, the Big Data collection is designed to empower your readers with actionable insights, emerging trends, and a comprehensive view of the future of data. If you're looking to understand and apply the power of Big Data to grow professionally or transform your business, this collection is for you. Available on Amazon, it is the essential guide to mastering the impact of data in the digital age.

10.2   Get to know the books in the Collection.

10.2.1 Simplifying Big Data into 7 Chapters.

This book is an essential guide for anyone who wants to understand and apply the fundamental concepts of Big Data in a clear and practical way. In a straightforward and accessible format, the book covers everything from theoretical pillars, such as the 5 Vs of Big Data, to modern tools and techniques, including Hadoop and Big Data Analytics.

Exploring real examples and strategies applicable in areas such as health, retail, and the environment, this work is ideal for technology professionals, managers, entrepreneurs, and students looking to transform data into valuable insights.

With an approach that connects theory and practice, this book is the perfect starting point for mastering the Big Data universe and leveraging its possibilities.

10.2.2 Big Data Management.

This book offers a practical and comprehensive approach to serving a diverse audience, from beginner analysts to experienced managers, students, and entrepreneurs.

With a focus on the efficient management of large volumes of information, this book presents in-depth analysis, real-world examples, comparisons between technologies such as Hadoop and Apache Spark, and practical strategies to avoid pitfalls and drive success.

Each chapter is structured to provide applicable insights, from the fundamentals to advanced analytics tools.

10.2.3 Big Data Architecture.

This book is intended for a diverse audience, including data architects who need to build robust platforms, analysts who want to understand how data layers integrate, and executives who are looking to inform informed decisions. Students and researchers in computer science, data engineering, and management will also find here a solid and up-to-date reference.

The content combines a practical approach and conceptual rigor. You'll be guided from the fundamentals, such as the 5 Vs of Big Data, to the complexity of layered architectures, spanning infrastructure, security, analytics tools, and storage standards like Data Lake and Data Warehouse.

In addition, clear examples, real case studies, and technology comparisons will help turn theoretical knowledge into practical applications and effective strategies.

10.2.4 Big Data Implementation.

This volume has been carefully crafted to be a practical and accessible guide, connecting theory to practice for professionals and students who want to master the strategic implementation of Big Data solutions.

It covers everything from quality analysis and data integration to topics such as real-time processing, virtualization, security, and governance, offering clear and applicable examples.

10.2.5 Strategies to Reduce Costs and Maximize Big Data Investments.

With a practical and reasoned approach, this book offers detailed analysis, real case studies and strategic solutions for IT managers, data analysts, entrepreneurs and business professionals.

This book is an indispensable guide to understanding and optimizing the costs associated with implementing Big Data, covering everything from storage and processing to small business-specific strategies and cloud cost analysis.

As part of the "Big Data" collection, it connects to other volumes that deeply explore the technical and strategic dimensions of the field, forming an essential library for anyone seeking to master the challenges and opportunities of the digital age.

10.2.6 700 Big Data Questions Collection.

This collection is designed to provide dynamic, challenging, and hands-on learning. With 700 questions strategically crafted and distributed in 5 volumes, it allows you to advance in the domain of Big Data in a progressive and engaging way. Each answer is an opportunity to expand your vision and apply concepts realistically and effectively.

The collection consists of the following books:

1   BIG DATA: 700 Questions - Volume 1.

It deals with information as the raw material for everything, the fundamental concepts and applications of Big Data.

2   BIG DATA: 700 Questions - Volume 2.

It addresses Big Data in the context of information science, data technology trends and analytics, Augmented analytics, continuous intelligence, distributed computing, and latency.

3   BIG DATA: 700 Questions - Volume 3.

It contemplates the technological and management aspects of Big Data, data mining, classification trees, logistic regression and professions in the context of Big Data.

4   BIG DATA: 700 Questions - Volume 4.

It deals with the requirements for Big Data management, the data structures used, the architecture and storage layers, Business Intelligence in the context of Big Data, and application virtualization.

5   BIG DATA: 700 Questions - Volume 5.

The book deals with SAAS, IAAS AND PAAS, Big Data implementation, overhead and hidden costs, Big Data for small businesses, digital security and data warehousing in the context of Big Data.

10.2.7 Big Data Glossary.

As large-scale data becomes the heart of strategic decisions in a variety of industries, this book offers a bridge between technical jargon and practical clarity, allowing you to turn complex information into valuable insights.

With clear definitions, practical examples, and intuitive organization, this glossary is designed to cater to a wide range of readers – from developers and data engineers to managers and the curious looking to explore the transformative impact of Big Data in their fields.

11 Discover the "Artificial Intelligence and the Power of Data" Collection – An Invitation to Transform Your Career and Knowledge.

The "Artificial Intelligence and the Power of Data" Collection was created for those who want not only to understand Artificial Intelligence (AI), but also to apply it strategically and practically.

In a series of carefully crafted volumes, I unravel complex concepts in a clear and accessible manner, ensuring the reader has a thorough understanding of AI and its impact on modern societies.

No matter what your level of familiarity with the topic, this collection turns the difficult into the didactic, the theoretical into the applicable, and the technical into something powerful for your career.

11.1   Why buy this collection?

We are living through an unprecedented technological revolution, where AI is the driving force in areas such as medicine, finance, education, government, and entertainment.

The collection "Artificial Intelligence and the Power of Data" dives deep into all these sectors, with practical examples and reflections that go far beyond traditional concepts.

You'll find both the technical expertise and the ethical and social implications of AI encouraging you to see this technology not just as a tool, but as a true agent of transformation.

Each volume is a fundamental piece of this innovative puzzle: from machine learning to data governance and from ethics to practical application.

With the guidance of an experienced author who combines academic research with years of hands-on practice, this collection is more than a set of books – it's an indispensable guide for anyone looking to navigate and excel in this burgeoning field.

11.2   Target Audience of this Collection?

This collection is for everyone who wants to play a prominent role in the age of AI:

- ✓ Tech Professionals: Receive deep technical insights to expand their skills.

- ✓ Students and the Curious: have access to clear explanations that facilitate the understanding of the complex universe of AI.

- ✓ Managers, business leaders, and policymakers will also benefit from the strategic vision on AI, which is essential for making well-informed decisions.

- ✓ Professionals in Career Transition: Professionals in career transition or interested in specializing in AI will find here complete material to build their learning trajectory.

11.3   Much More Than Technique – A Complete Transformation.

This collection is not just a series of technical books; It is a tool for intellectual and professional growth.

With it, you go far beyond theory: each volume invites you to a deep reflection on the future of humanity in a world where machines and algorithms are increasingly present.

This is your invitation to master the knowledge that will define the future and become part of the transformation that Artificial Intelligence brings to the world.

Be a leader in your industry, master the skills the market demands, and prepare for the future with the "Artificial Intelligence and the Power of Data" collection.

This is not just a purchase; It is a decisive investment in your learning and professional development journey.

12 The Books of the Collection.

12.1 Data, Information and Knowledge in the era of Artificial Intelligence.

This book essentially explores the theoretical and practical foundations of Artificial Intelligence, from data collection to its transformation into intelligence. It focuses primarily on machine learning, AI training, and neural networks.

12.2 From Data to Gold: How to Turn Information into Wisdom in the Age of AI.

This book offers a critical analysis on the evolution of Artificial Intelligence, from raw data to the creation of artificial wisdom, integrating neural networks, deep learning, and knowledge modeling.

It presents practical examples in health, finance, and education, and addresses ethical and technical challenges.

12.3 Challenges and Limitations of Data in AI.

The book offers an in-depth analysis of the role of data in the development of AI exploring topics such as quality, bias, privacy, security, and scalability with practical case studies in healthcare, finance, and public safety.

12.4   Historical Data in Databases for AI: Structures, Preservation, and Purge.

This book investigates how historical data management is essential to the success of AI projects. It addresses the relevance of ISO standards to ensure quality and safety, in addition to analyzing trends and innovations in data processing.

12.5   Controlled Vocabulary for Data Dictionary: A Complete Guide.

This comprehensive guide explores the advantages and challenges of implementing controlled vocabularies in the context of AI and information science. With a detailed approach, it covers everything from the naming of data elements to the interactions between semantics and cognition.

12.6   Data Curation and Management for the Age of AI.

This book presents advanced strategies for transforming raw data into valuable insights, with a focus on meticulous curation and efficient data management. In addition to technical solutions, it addresses ethical and legal issues, empowering the reader to face the complex challenges of information.

12.7   Information Architecture.

The book addresses data management in the digital age, combining theory and practice to create efficient and scalable AI systems, with insights into modeling and ethical and legal challenges.

12.8   Fundamentals: The Essentials of Mastering Artificial Intelligence.

An essential work for anyone who wants to master the key concepts of AI, with an accessible approach and practical examples. The book explores innovations such as Machine Learning and Natural Language

Processing, as well as ethical and legal challenges, and offers a clear view of the impact of AI on various industries.

12.9   LLMS - Large-Scale Language Models.

This essential guide helps you understand the revolution of Large-Scale Language Models (LLMs) in AI.

The book explores the evolution of GPTs and the latest innovations in human-computer interaction, offering practical insights into their impact on industries such as healthcare, education, and finance.

12.10   Machine Learning: Fundamentals and Advances.

This book offers a comprehensive overview of supervised and unsupervised algorithms, deep neural networks, and federated learning. In addition to addressing issues of ethics and explainability of models.

12.11   Inside Synthetic Minds.

This book reveals how these 'synthetic minds' are redefining creativity, work, and human interactions. This work presents a detailed analysis of the challenges and opportunities provided by these technologies, exploring their profound impact on society.

12.12   The Issue of Copyright.

This book invites the reader to explore the future of creativity in a world where human-machine collaboration is a reality, addressing questions about authorship, originality, and intellectual property in the age of generative AIs.

12.13   1121 Questions and Answers: From Basic to Complex – Part 1 to 4.

Organized into four volumes, these questions serve as essential practical guides to mastering key AI concepts.

Part 1 addresses information, data, geoprocessing, the evolution of artificial intelligence, its historical milestones and basic concepts.

Part 2 delves into complex concepts such as machine learning, natural language processing, computer vision, robotics, and decision algorithms.

Part 3 addresses issues such as data privacy, work automation, and the impact of large-scale language models (LLMs).

Part 4 explores the central role of data in the age of artificial intelligence, delving into the fundamentals of AI and its applications in areas such as mental health, government, and anti-corruption.

12.14 The Definitive Glossary of Artificial Intelligence.

This glossary presents more than a thousand artificial intelligence concepts clearly explained, covering topics such as Machine Learning, Natural Language Processing, Computer Vision, and AI Ethics.

- Part 1 contemplates concepts starting with the letters A to D.
- Part 2 contemplates concepts initiated by the letters E to M.
- Part 3 contemplates concepts starting with the letters N to Z.

12.15 Prompt Engineering - Volumes 1 to 6.

This collection covers all the fundamentals of prompt engineering, providing a complete foundation for professional development.

With a rich variety of prompts for areas such as leadership, digital marketing, and information technology, it offers practical examples to improve clarity, decision-making, and gain valuable insights.

The volumes cover the following subjects:

- Volume 1: Fundamentals. Structuring Concepts and History of Prompt Engineering.
- Volume 2: Security and Privacy in AI.

- Volume 3: Language Models, Tokenization, and Training Methods.
- Volume 4: How to Ask Right Questions.
- Volume 5: Case Studies and Errors.
- Volume 6: The Best Prompts.

12.16   Guide to Being a Prompt Engineer – Volumes 1 and 2.

The collection explores the advanced fundamentals and skills required to be a successful prompt engineer, highlighting the benefits, risks, and the critical role this role plays in the development of artificial intelligence.

Volume 1 covers crafting effective prompts, while Volume 2 is a guide to understanding and applying the fundamentals of Prompt Engineering.

12.17   Data Governance with AI – Volumes 1 to 3.

Find out how to implement effective data governance with this comprehensive collection. Offering practical guidance, this collection covers everything from data architecture and organization to protection and quality assurance, providing a complete view to transform data into strategic assets.

Volume 1 addresses practices and regulations. Volume 2 explores in depth the processes, techniques, and best practices for conducting effective audits on data models. Volume 3 is your definitive guide to deploying data governance with AI.

12.18   Algorithm Governance.

This book looks at the impact of algorithms on society, exploring their foundations and addressing ethical and regulatory issues. It addresses transparency, accountability, and bias, with practical solutions for auditing and monitoring algorithms in sectors such as finance, health, and education.

12.19 From IT Professional to AI Expert: The Ultimate Guide to a Successful Career Transition.

For Information Technology professionals, the transition to AI represents a unique opportunity to enhance skills and contribute to the development of innovative solutions that shape the future.

In this book, we investigate the reasons for making this transition, the essential skills, the best learning path, and the prospects for the future of the IT job market.

12.20 Intelligent Leadership with AI: Transform Your Team and Drive Results.

This book reveals how artificial intelligence can revolutionize team management and maximize organizational performance.

By combining traditional leadership techniques with AI-powered insights, such as predictive analytics-based leadership, you'll learn how to optimize processes, make more strategic decisions, and create more efficient and engaged teams.

12.21 Impacts and Transformations: Complete Collection.

This collection offers a comprehensive and multifaceted analysis of the transformations brought about by Artificial Intelligence in contemporary society.

- Volume 1: Challenges and Solutions in the Detection of Texts Generated by Artificial Intelligence.
- Volume 2: The Age of Filter Bubbles. Artificial Intelligence and the Illusion of Freedom.
- Volume 3: Content Creation with AI - How to Do It?
- Volume 4: The Singularity Is Closer Than You Think.
- Volume 5: Human Stupidity versus Artificial Intelligence.

- Volume 6: The Age of Stupidity! A Cult of Stupidity?
- Volume 7: Autonomy in Motion: The Intelligent Vehicle Revolution.
- Volume 8: Poiesis and Creativity with AI.
- Volume 9: Perfect Duo: AI + Automation.
- Volume 10: Who Holds the Power of Data?

12.22   Big Data with AI: Complete Collection.

The collection covers everything from the technological fundamentals and architecture of Big Data to the administration and glossary of essential technical terms.

The collection also discusses the future of humanity's relationship with the enormous volume of data generated in the databases of training in Big Data structuring.

- Volume 1: Fundamentals.
- Volume 2: Architecture.
- Volume 3: Implementation.
- Volume 4: Administration.
- Volume 5: Essential Themes and Definitions.
- Volume 6: Data Warehouse, Big Data, and AI.

13 About the Author.

I'm Marcus Pinto, better known as Prof. Marcão, a specialist in information technology, information architecture and artificial intelligence.

With more than four decades of dedicated work and research, I have built a solid and recognized trajectory, always focused on making technical knowledge accessible and applicable to all those who seek to understand and stand out in this transformative field.

My experience spans strategic consulting, education and authorship, as well as an extensive performance as an information architecture analyst.

This experience enables me to offer innovative solutions adapted to the constantly evolving needs of the technological market, anticipating trends and creating bridges between technical knowledge and practical impact.

Over the years, I have developed comprehensive and in-depth expertise in data, artificial intelligence, and information governance –

areas that have become essential for building robust and secure systems capable of handling the vast volume of data that shapes today's world.

My book collection, available on Amazon, reflects this expertise, addressing topics such as Data Governance, Big Data, and Artificial Intelligence with a clear focus on practical applications and strategic vision.

Author of more than 150 books, I investigate the impact of artificial intelligence in multiple spheres, exploring everything from its technical bases to the ethical issues that become increasingly urgent with the adoption of this technology on a large scale.

In my lectures and mentorships, I share not only the value of AI, but also the challenges and responsibilities that come with its implementation – elements that I consider essential for ethical and conscious adoption.

I believe that technological evolution is an inevitable path. My books are a proposed guide on this path, offering deep and accessible insights for those who want not only to understand, but to master the technologies of the future.

With a focus on education and human development, I invite you to join me on this transformative journey, exploring the possibilities and challenges that this digital age has in store for us.

14 How to Contact Prof. Marcão.

14.1   For lectures, training and business mentoring.

marcao.tecno@gmail.com

14.2   Prof. Marcão, on Linkedin.

https://bit.ly/linkedin_profmarcao

www.ingramcontent.com/pod-product-compliance
Lightning Source LLC
LaVergne TN
LVHW022350060326
832902LV00022B/4361